Getting Along

Activities for Teaching Cooperation, Responsibility and Respect

Dianne Schilling

Innerchoice Publishing, Torrance, California 90505

Cover Design: Doug Armstrong Graphic Design
Illustrations: Dianne Schilling

ISBN: 1-56499-012-5

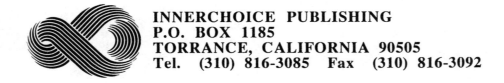

INNERCHOICE PUBLISHING
P.O. BOX 1185
TORRANCE, CALIFORNIA 90505
Tel. (310) 816-3085 Fax (310) 816-3092

What everybody already knows—
whether they are
in gradeschool or a rest home,
a banker or a migrant farmer,
beautiful or plain,
a college graduate or a dropout,
unemployed or financially independent,
German, English, Peruvian,
Indonesian, Angolian, South African,
Tibetan, Lebanese, Iranian or American—
is that we are meant to live in peace.

—Thomas Pettepiece
What Everybody Already Knows:
A Book About Peacemaking

Jalmar Press and Innerchoice Publishing are happy to announce

a collaborative effort under which all Innerchoice titles will now be distributed

only through Jalmar Press.

To request the latest catalog of our joint resources for use by teachers, counselors

and other care-givers to empower children to develop inner-directed living and

learning skills

call us at: (800) 662-9662

or fax us at: (310) 816-3092

or send us a card at: P.O. Box 1185, Torrance, CA 90505

We're eager to serve you and the students you work with.

By the way, Jalmar Press has several new titles coming up that can give you all
the necessary tools to teach conflict resolution to all your students. One of the
new products is called
THE PEACEFUL CLASSROOM IN ACTION, by Naomi Drew
It shows how Learning the Skills of Peacemaking, Naomi's first book, has
effectively been used in the classroom over the past 11 years. It is aimed at
grades K - 6.

A second title is
NONVIOLENT COMMUNICATION: A Language of Compassion by
Dr. Marshall B. Rosenberg
The dynamic communication techniques that Dr. Rosenberg has developed
transform potential conflicts into peaceful dialogues. Outstanding simple tools to
defuse arguments. Applicable K - Adult.

Write or call for the latest information or to place your order.

Contents

Introduction

What does it take for people to get along? What is required for individuals and groups from diverse backgrounds to willingly seek common ground while respecting and proudly maintaining the sundry paths that brought them to the places they share?

Our multicultural society is made up almost exclusively of immigrants and the descendents of immigrants, many of whom arrived on these shores seeking religious tolerance and freedom from oppression. What ethics must we nourish in our children, what skills do our youth need to learn in order to appreciate the brilliant kaleidoscope of colors and cultures they have inherited? How can we get them to honor, enjoy, and protect what increasing numbers would shatter and separate into little piles of hues and textures with jagged, hostile edges?

We can start by recognizing that a school is a community and the classroom a smaller community, and that whatever happens here not only goes home, but to the theater, the mall, the library, the park, the athletic event, and the religious service. Children must grasp that in order for *any* of us to truly enjoy and benefit from the amenities and opportunities that are available in the community, in order for *any* of us to feel entirely safe and secure, in order for *any* of us to expect optimal conditions for learning and growth, we must ensure that those same benefits, securities, and conditions are available to *all* of us. In short, we must learn to get along. We don't always have to agree. We can expect to have different ideas, different values, and different goals, but we must learn to respect one another's rights, to work and play cooperatively, to resolve conflicts, and to take responsibility for our own behaviors and the effects those have on others and on the community as a whole.

Merely admonishing students to be "good citizens" is not enough. Most are very familiar with the label and can readily parrot all the implied expectations. For students to get along in the deeper sense characterized by true interdependence, they have to develop self-awareness; undertake responsibility for their actions; accept and appreciate differences in others; listen with empathy and understanding; communicate their thoughts and feelings accurately and assertively; include others in their activities; be open to divergent styles and points of view; work together to solve problems and complete projects; and peacefully resolve any conflicts they experience along the way. What's more, they have to be conscious that they are doing these things, and be able to verbalize the reasons and benefits. To develop competency in these areas involves the acquisition of specific skills, along with growing awareness and open discussion concerning the process. This in turn requires not just explanation, but modeling, plenty of practice or behavioral rehearsal, and ongoing dialogue.

The activities in *Getting Along* are designed to introduce (or reintroduce) students to these skills in a deliberate, enjoyable fashion and, in the process, elevate their awareness of the responsibility that each has to make the classroom and/or school a cooperative environment where everyone is included, where people experience true interdependence, and where dissent and conflict are never fearsome or ugly but, rather, natural and productive.

Notice that the operative word is "introduce." There aren't nearly enough activities in this book to complete the task of skill development. Moreover, as a teacher or counselor, you know that students are confronted daily with numerous real-life incidents whose potential for teaching these same skills is greater than any curriculum can offer, precisely because the incidents are real and immediate. What this book offers — through role plays, games, simulations, and discussions — is sufficient preparation to allow students to carry over their awareness and responsible attitudes to life's thousand-and-one daily challenges where, with guidance and feedback, they can continue to hone their skills.

Getting Along is not the complete answer, but it is a great place to start.

How To Use the Activities

The activities in *Getting Along* are grouped into seven topic areas:

- Appreciating Differences
- Communicating Effectively
- Developing Friendship Skills
- Helping and Being Helped
- Including Others
- Resolving Conflicts
- Working Together

Although topic areas, and activities within topic areas, are arranged in a developmental sequence, you are free to implement activities in any order you choose. For example, if you are particularly concerned about the exclusion of certain students from group activities, you might want to skip from "Appreciating Differences" to "Including Others." If a serious conflict erupts in the classroom, by all means take advantage of the opportunity to introduce strategies from "Resolving Conflicts."

The final topic area, "Working Together," includes several simulations that offer students the opportunity to practice many of the skills introduced in earlier activities. Implementing an activity such as "Stepping Stones" or "Connect" early will have the effect of a pretest — raising student awareness of the importance of such things as communication, cooperation, inclusion, and conflict resolution, and of their strengths and weaknesses in these areas. If you use an activity in this manner, be sure to repeat the same or a similar activity several weeks or months later so students can measure and appreciate their skill development and personal growth.

Many of the activities in *Getting Along* are accompanied by *experience sheets*; instructions for the use of these handouts are included in the activity directions. Experience sheets promote individual awareness and reflection, and are never collected or graded — although students may be asked to discuss learnings derived from experience sheets with their classmates.

At the conclusion of most activities, you will find a list of discussion questions. Always try to allow enough time to facilitate a brief summary discussion. Students benefit most from an activity when they are given the opportunity to talk about the experience immediately afterwards, verbalizing their insights and making connections to events and conditions in their lives. Feel free to substitute questions that have greater relevancy to issues the students are dealing with in the classroom, school, or community. Do not use the summary discussion to sermonize or lecture, or to force connections that the students are not ready to make. Do keep the questions open-ended (requiring more than a "yes" or "no" response), attempt to stimulate higher-level thinking, and facilitate, facilitate, facilitate.

The Circle Session

The final activities in each topic area are *circle sessions*. A circle session is a small-group discussion characterized by a unique two-part structure (sharing followed by summary discussion) and prescribed rules of conduct that ensure acceptance, listening, safety, mutual respect, and confidentiality.

The value of the circle session lies in the fact that it is guided by an established procedure and a specific topic. Every student is given uninterrupted time to respond to the topic while everyone else listens attentively. Open dialogue follows only after every circle member has accepted or declined this opportunity.

The sharing and discussion phases of the circle are procedurally and qualitatively different, yet of equal importance. This is perhaps the trickiest distinction for a new circle leader to make. During the sharing phase, circle members voluntarily share their feelings, ideas, and insights concerning the topic. Only after *all members* have shared does the leader open up the circle to the give and take of general discussion. The longer you lead and participate in circles, the more you will appreciate the benefits of maintaining the integrity of these two phases.

The following sections cover everything you need to know about leading circle sessions.

Setting Up Circle Sessions

Group Size and Composition

Circle sessions are a time for focusing on individuals' contributions in an unhurried fashion. For this reason, each circle session group needs to be kept relatively small — eight to twelve usually works best. Students at this age are capable of extensive verbalization. You will want to encourage this, and not stifle them because of time constraints.

Each group should be as **heterogeneous** as possible with respect to sex, ability, and racial/ethnic background. Sometimes there will be a group in which all the students are particularly reticent to speak. At these times, bring in an expressive student or two who will get things going. Sometimes it is necessary for practical reasons to change the membership of a group. Once established, however, it is advisable to keep a group as stable as possible.

Length and Location of Circle sessions

Most circle sessions last approximately 20 to 30 minutes. At first students tend to be reluctant to express themselves fully because they do not yet know that the circle is a safe place. Consequently your first sessions may not last more than 10 to 15 minutes. Generally speaking, students become comfortable and motivated to speak with continued experience.

In secondary classrooms, circle sessions may be conducted at any time during the class period. Starting circle sessions at the beginning of the period allows additional time in case students become deeply involved in the topic. If you start circles late in the period, make sure the students are aware of their responsibility to be concise.

In elementary classes, any time of day is appropriate for circle sessions. Some teachers like to set the tone for the day by beginning with circles; others feel it's a perfect way to complete the day and to send the children away with positive feelings.

Circle sessions may be carried out wherever there is room for students to sit in a circle and experience few or no distractions. Most leaders prefer to have students sit in chairs rather than on the floor. Students are less apt to invade one another's space while seated in chairs. Some leaders conduct sessions outdoors, with students seated in a secluded, grassy area.

How to Get Started

Teachers and counselors have used numerous methods to involve students in the circle process. What works well for one leader or class does not always work for another. Here are two basic strategies leaders have successfully used to set up groups. Whichever you use, we recommend that you post a chart listing the circle session rules and procedures to which participants may refer.

1. Start one group at a time, and cycle through all groups. Students who are not participating may work on course work or silent reading, or, if you have a cooperative librarian, they may be sent to the library to work independently or in small groups on a class assignment. Repeat this procedure until all of the students have been involved in at least one circle session. Then initiate a class discussion in which you explain that from now on you will be meeting with each circle group in the classroom, with the remainder of the class present. Ask the students to help you plan established procedures for the remainder of the class to follow. Thereafter, meet with each circle session group on a different day.

2. Combine inner and outer circles. Meet with one circle session group while the other groups listen and observe as a combined outer circle. *Invite the members of the outer circle to participate in the review and discussion phases of the circle.* If you run out of time in secondary classrooms, use two class periods for this. On succeeding days, repeat the procedure — each time with a different circle session group comprising the inner circle.

Leading the Circle Session

This section is a thorough guide for conducting circle sessions. Please remember that these guidelines are presented to assist you, not to restrict you. Follow them and trust your own leadership style at the same time.

```
Circle Session Leader Procedures
Setting up the circle  (1-2 minutes)
Reviewing the ground rules  (1-2 minutes) *
Introducing the topic  (1-2 minutes)
Sharing by circle members  (12-18 minutes)
Reviewing what is shared  (3-5 minutes) **
Summary discussion  (2-8 minutes)
Closing the circle  (less than 1 minute)

*optional after the first few sessions   **optional
```

Setting up the circle (1-2 minutes)

As you sit down with the students in the circle, remember that you are not teaching a lesson. You are facilitating a group of people. Establish a positive atmosphere. In a relaxed manner, address each student by name, using eye contact and conveying warmth. An attitude of seriousness blended with enthusiasm will let the students know that the circle session is an important learning experience — an activity that can be interesting and meaningful.

Reviewing the ground rules (1-2 minutes).

At the beginning of the first session, and at appropriate intervals thereafter, go over the rules for the circle session. They are:

```
Circle Session Rules
1. Bring yourself to the circle and nothing else.
2. Everyone gets a turn to share, including the
   leader.
3. You can skip your turn if you wish.
4. Listen to the person who is sharing.
5. The time is shared equally.
6. Stay in your own space.
7. There are no interruptions, probing,
   put-downs, or gossip.
```

From this point on, demonstrate to the students that you expect them to remember and abide by the rules. Convey that you think well of them and know they are fully capable of responsible behavior. Let them know that by coming to the session they are making a commitment to listen and show acceptance and respect for the other students and you.

Introducing the topic (1-2 minutes)

State the topic in your own words. Elaborate and provide examples as each activity suggests. Add clarifying statements of your own that will help the students understand the topic. Answer questions about the topic, and emphasize that there are no "right" responses. Finally, restate the topic, opening the session to responses (theirs and yours). Sometimes taking your turn first helps the students understand the aim of the topic. At various points throughout the session, state the topic again.

Just prior to leading a circle session, contemplate the topic and think of at least one possible response that *you* can make.

Sharing by circle members (12-18 minutes)

The most important point to remember is this: The purpose of the circle session is to give students an opportunity to express themselves and be accepted for the experiences, thoughts, and feelings they share. Avoid taking the action away from the circle members. They are the stars!

Reviewing what is shared (optional 3-5 minutes)

Besides modeling effective listening (the very best way to teach it) and positively reinforcing students for attentive listening, a review can be used to deliberately improve listening skills in circle members.

Reviewing is a time for reflective listening, when circle members feed back what they heard each other say during the sharing phase of the circle. Besides encouraging effective listening, reviewing provides circle members with additional recognition. It validates their experience and conveys the idea, "you are important," a message we can all profit from hearing often.

To review, a circle member simply addresses someone who shared, and briefly paraphrases what the person said ("John, I heard you say....").

The first few times you conduct reviews, stress the importance of checking with the speaker to see if the review accurately summarized the main things that were shared. If the speaker says, "No," allow him or her to make corrections. Stress too, the importance of speaking *directly* to the speaker, using the person's name and the pronoun "you," not "he" or "she." If someone says, "She said that...," intervene as promptly and respectfully as possible and say to the reviewer, "Talk to Betty...Say you." This is very important. The person whose turn is being reviewed will have a totally different feeling when talked *to*, instead of *about*.

Note: Remember that the review is optional and is most effective when used occasionally, not as a part of every circle.

Summary discussion (2-8 minutes)

The summary discussion is the cognitive portion of the circle session. During this phase, the leader asks thought-provoking questions to stimulate free discussion and higher-level thinking. Each circle session in this book includes summary questions; however, at times you may want to formulate questions that are more appropriate to the level of understanding in your group — or to what was actually shared in the circle. If you wish to make connections between the circle session topic and your content area, ask questions that will accomplish that objective and allow the summary discussion to extend longer.

It is important that you not confuse the summary with the review. The review is optional; the summary is not. The summary meets the need of people of all ages to find meaning in what they do. Thus, the summary serves as a necessary culmination to each circle session by allowing the students to clarify the key concepts they gained from the session.

Closing the circle (less than 1 minute).

The ideal time to end a circle session is when the summary discussion reaches natural closure. Sincerely thank everyone for being part of the circle. Don't thank specific students for speaking, as doing so might convey the impression that speaking is more appreciated than mere listening. Then close the circle by saying, "The circle session is over," or "OK, that ends our session."

More about Circle Sessions

The next few paragraphs offer further clarification concerning circle session leadership.

Why should students bring themselves to the circle and nothing else? Individual teachers differ on this point, but most prefer that students not bring objects (such as pencils, books, etc.) to the circle that may be distracting.

Who gets to talk? Everyone (including you). The importance of acceptance in circle sessions cannot be overly stressed. In one way or another practically every ground rule says one thing: *accept one another.* When you model acceptance of students, they will learn how to be accepting. Each individual in the circle is important and deserves a turn to speak if he or she wishes to take it. Equal opportunity to become involved should be given to everyone in the circle.

Does everyone have to take a turn? No. Students may choose to skip their turns. If the circle becomes a pressure situation in which the members are coerced in any way to speak, it will become an unsafe place where participants are not comfortable. Meaningful discussion is unlikely in such an atmosphere. By allowing students to make this choice, you are showing them that you accept their right to remain silent if that is what they choose to do.

Sometimes a silence occurs during a circle session. Don't feel you have to jump in every time someone stops talking. During silences students have an opportunity to think about what they would like to share or to contemplate an important idea they've heard. A general rule of thumb is to allow silence to the point that you observe group discomfort. At that point move on. *Do not switch to another topic.* To do so implies you will not be satisfied until the students speak.

How can I encourage effective listening? In the circle session, listening is defined as the respectful focusing of attention on individual speakers. It includes eye contact with the speaker and open body posture. It eschews interruptions of any kind. When you conduct a circle session, listen and encourage listening in the students by (l) focusing your attention on the person who is speaking, (2) being receptive to what the speaker is saying (not mentally planning your next remark), and (3) recognizing the speaker when she finishes speaking, either verbally ("Thanks, Shirley") or nonverbally (a nod and a smile).

No one was born knowing how to listen effectively to others. It is a skill like any other that gets better as it is practiced. To encourage effective listening in the students, reinforce them by letting them know you have noticed they were listening to each other and appreciate it. Occasionally conducting a review after the sharing phase also has the effect of sharpening listening skills.

How can I ensure the students get equal time? Be very clear with the students about the purpose of this ground rule. Tell them at the outset how much time there is and whether or not you plan to conduct a review. When it is your turn, always limit your own contribution. If someone goes on and on, do intervene (dominators need to know what they are doing), but do so as respectfully as you can.

What are some examples of put-downs? Put-downs convey the message, "You are not okay as you are." Some put-downs are deliberate, but many are made unknowingly. Both kinds are undesirable in a circle session because they destroy the atmosphere of acceptance and disrupt the flow of discussion. Typical put-downs include:

- overquestioning.
- statements that have the effect of teaching or preaching
- advice giving
- one-upsmanship
- criticism, disapproval, or objections
- sarcasm
- statements or questions of disbelief

How can I deal with put-downs? There are two major ways for dealing with put-downs in circle sessions: preventing them from occurring and intervening when they do.

Going over the ground rules with the students at the beginning of each session, particularly in the earliest sessions, is a helpful preventive technique. Another is to reinforce the students when they adhere to the rule. Be sure to use nonpatronizing, nonevaluative language.

Unacceptable behavior should be stopped the moment it is recognized by the leader. When you become aware that a put-down is occurring, do whatever you ordinarily do to stop destructive behavior in the classroom. If one student gives another an unasked-for bit of advice, say, for example, "Jane, please give Alicia a chance to tell her story." To a student who interrupts, say, "Ed, it's Sally's turn." In most cases the fewer words, the better — students automatically tune out messages delivered as lectures.

Sometimes students disrupt the group by starting a private conversation with the person next to them. Touch the offender on the arm or shoulder while continuing to give eye contact to the student who is speaking. If you can't reach the offender, simply remind him or her of the rule about listening. If students persist in putting others down during circle sessions, ask to see them at another time and hold a brief one-to-one conference, urging them to follow the rules. Suggest that they reconsider their membership in the circle. Make it clear that if they don't intend to honor the ground rules, they are not to come to the circle.

How can I keep students from gossiping? Periodically remind students that using names and sharing embarrassing information is not acceptable. Urge the students to relate personally to one another, but not to tell intimate details of their lives.

What should the leader do during the summary discussion? Conduct the summary as an open forum, giving students the opportunity to discuss a variety of ideas and accept those that make sense to them. Don't impose your opinions on the students, or allow the students to impose theirs on one another. Ask open-ended questions, encourage higher-level thinking, contribute your own ideas when appropriate, and act as a facilitator.

Are We the Same or Different?
Presentation and Group Discussion

Objectives:
The students will:
—name specific ways in which people are different and the same.
—demonstrate that individual perception determines whether a characteristic is seen as a difference or a commonality.
—recognize commonalties as vital to achieving understanding and harmony.
—describe differences as vital to achieving success.

Materials:
chalkboard or chart paper

Directions:
Draw a horizontal line on the chalkboard, dividing a section of the board approximately in half. At the top of the board, write the heading, "Different." Begin the activity by asking the students to name all of the ways that human beings differ from one another. Write their suggestions below the heading. You will probably list such items as personality, preferences, skills, intelligence, traditions, culture, race, gender, abilities, physical appearance, socioeconomic status, etc. Keep going until the space above the line is crowded with items.

Write the heading, "Same," at the top of the lower section of board, just below the line. Ask the students to name all of the ways in which humans are *exactly* the same. Suggestions will come more slowly this time. Be patient and see if someone comes up with the idea that all the items written above the line also represent ways in which people are exactly alike. (The idea is that *all* people possess personalities, skills, intelligence, etc., even though these attributes differ qualitatively from one person to another. In fact, this can be said for every item written above the line. All of these things not only make people different, they also make them the same.) If one of the students makes this observation, proceed from there. If no one discovers the concept, explain that you can add greatly to the list, and begin underlining items above the line, saying something like, "We all have different personalities, but we all have a personality, etc." Make the point that people are as much alike as they are different.

Explain that whether we see these items as differences or commonalties depends on our perception. When we focus only on the ways we differ, we tend to grow apart, but when we focus on commonalties, we tend to come together. This coming together creates strength in diversity. It can be thought of, too, as *unity through diversity* or *common ground*.

Tell the students that ALL successful teams are built on diversity. Using the example of personalities, demonstrate how everyone on a team has an individual personality, and that together those personalities make up the team personality. Members have different talents, skills, and knowledge to bring to a team. These differences are what make teams strong. Without diversity, a team cannot have much strength.

When individuals believe that their differences make them right or better (and make others wrong or worse, conflicts occur. The need to see our differences as "right" or "wrong" destroys our ability to work together effectively.

Discussion Questions:
1. What are some ways in which all people benefit from individual differences?
2. How can differences among group members contribute to their efforts when working on a joint endeavor?
3. How does the need to be "right" interfere with efforts to build on diversity?

Counting on Each Other
Experience Sheet and Discussion

Objectives:
The students will:
—identify specific ways in which people "count on" one another.
—name specific ways in which they count on individual classmates.
—explain why it is important for people to rely on one another.
—define t*rust* and explain how it develops.

Materials:
one copy of the experience sheet, "Count on Me" for each student; chalkboard and chalk

Directions:
Ask the students to help you brainstorm some of the many different ways people count on one another in the classroom and elsewhere. List their ideas on the chalkboard or chart paper. To facilitate, ask such questions as, "What do we count on each other for?" "What do you count on me for?" "What do you count on your parents for?" "What do you count on your neighbors for?" "What do you count on your best friend for?" Write their ideas on the chalkboard. Include such items as:

I count on _____ to help me solve problems.
    ...spend leisure time with me.
    ...make me laugh.
    ...listen when I talk.
    ...keep a confidence.
    ...help with responsibilities at home.
    ...help with school assignments.
    ...tell the truth.
    ...understand me.
    ...answer my questions.
    ...love me.
    ...be fair in games and sports.
    ...protect me.
    ...do a good job.
    ...be on time.
    ...keep a promise.

Continued, next page

Distribute the experience sheets. Announce that you want the students to think about the unique qualities, talents, and abilities of each person in the class and write down one way in which they count on that person. Tell them to use the list on the board for ideas. If the group or class is very large, have the students complete this assignment in smaller groups. Existing work groups would be ideal.

When the students have finished, ask several students at a time to come to the front of the room. Refer to one student at a time and ask: "What do you count on (John) for?" Call on individual students to read what they have written. Repeat this process with the remainder of the students. Conclude with a class discussion.

Discussion Questions:
1. How do you feel knowing that you can count on so many people?
2. How do we learn to rely on other people?
3. How do you let others know they can count on you?
4. How does knowing you can count on someone build trust?

Count on Me!
Experience Sheet

I can count on _____ to _____

_____ .

I can count on _____ to _____

_____ .

I can count on _____ to _____

_____ .

I can count on _____ to _____

_____ .

I can count on _____ to _____

_____ .

I can count on _____ to _____

_____ .

I can count on _____ to _____

_____ .

I can count on _____ to _____

_____ .

I can count on _____ to _____

_____ .

I can count on _____ to _____

_____ .

My classmates can count on me to:

1. _____
   _____

2. _____
   _____

3. _____
   _____

In Search of the Perfect Person
Experiment and Discussion

Objectives:
The students will:
—state that there are no perfect people.
—identify examples of perfectionistic thinking.
—describe how perfectionism erodes self-esteem and esteem
   for others.
—challenge perfectionistic thinking in themselves and others.

Materials:
at least four of the following: pictures of Presidents of the United
States, movie stars, baseball players, or different types of dogs or
cats; collections of apples, pears, marbles, rocks, or other slightly
different items of the same class or type

Directions:
   Place the items chosen on a table and ask a few students at a
time to come up and examine them very carefully. After the students have had a chance to study the items, ask the following
questions (modified to suit the items chosen):

—*Which of the Presidents do you think was the most perfect
   President?*
—*Which one of the apples (pears, etc.) is the most perfect apple?*
—*Which one of the marbles (rocks, etc.) is the most perfect
   example of a marble?*
—*Which movie star is the most perfect of all movie stars?*

   Ask the students whether they know why they are attempting to
find the best example from the different groups of items. Elicit from
them the fact that there are many fine examples in each group, and
no one example is absolutely perfect.

   Point out that since being perfect is impossible (and not much
fun), it doesn't make sense for people to think that they and others
have to be perfect to be liked, successful, or happy. Ask the stu-

dents to share some perfectionistic ideas that might keep them from feeling good about themselves and others. For example:

- If I don't get all A's, I'm no good.
- If I'm not beautiful/handsome, no one will ever go out with me.
- If I'm clumsy, everyone will laugh at me.
- People in wheelchairs are confined and helpless.
- Fat people shouldn't wear shorts or bathing suits.
- People who don't have college degrees aren't very smart.

Bring up the idea that students can help one another develop positive self-esteem by challenging perfectionistic ideas in the group. For example:

- "Mike, just because you stutter sometimes doesn't mean you shouldn't try out for the debate team. Look how you make us all think and question!"
- "Cheryl, you seemed embarrassed after telling us you have epilepsy. It's difficult to let others know about things like that, but you're still the same person you've always been."
- "Ann, just because you're heavy doesn't mean you can't sing with a band. You have a terrific voice."

Ask whether the students are willing to challenge perfectionistic thinking in themselves and in other group members when they see it.

Discussion Questions:
1. How many perfect people have you met in your lifetime?
2. If you haven't met a perfect person, what do you think your chances are of meeting one in the future?
3. Do you think it is possible to be perfect? What would being perfect be like?
4. Do you think you were born with perfectionistic ideas, or did you learn them? If so, how did you learn them?
5. How is using a wheelchair or seeing-eye dog similar to using eye glasses or a hearing aid? How is it different? How does it compare with using a hairpiece, having cosmetic surgery, or wearing fancy clothes?

Success Bombardment
Experience Sheet and Group Exercise

Objectives:
The students will:
—recognize and describe their own worth and worthiness.
—identify strengths, talents, and special abilities in themselves and others.
—practice positive self-talk.

Note: For optimum impact, use this activity after your students have had time to develop as a group, e.g., have experienced several activities and circle sessions together.

Materials:
one copy of the experience sheet, "Success Inventory" for each student; 12 small self-adhesive labels per student; and 1 copy of the "Target" worksheet for each student

Directions:
Distribute the "Success Inventory" experience sheets. Go over the directions and answer any questions. Have the students work individually to fill out the sheets. Allow about 15 minutes. If the students appear to be having trouble thinking of accomplishments, take a couple of minutes and talk to the entire class about such examples as learning to: *walk, talk, dress, dance, play, sing, count, problem-solve, read, write, love; ride a bike, skateboard, roller-skate; ski, play softball, volleyball, soccer, basketball; cook, play an instrument, use a computer, be a friend, join an organization; earn a merit badge, award, or certificate; learn to type, baby-sit, care for a pet; etc., etc.*

When the students have completed their sheets, ask them to form groups of four or five. Give 12 small, blank, self-adhesive labels and a "Target" worksheet to each student.

Direct the students to take turns describing their accomplishments to the other members of their group. In your own words, explain: *Tell you group why you picked those particular successes. Explain how you felt about them at the time they occurred and why they are particularly meaningful to you now. Immediately after you share, the other members of your group will each make three labels that describe positive things about you based on the successes you shared. For example, the first person's labels might say, "industrious and energetic," "musically talented," and "born to lead." Then, while you hold up your "target," that person will look directly at you, tell you what he or she has written on each label, and stick the labels on your target. The other members of your group will then take a turn "bombarding" you with their success labels in the same manner. If there are three other people in your group (total of four), you will end up with nine labels on your target. A second person in the group will then take a turn reading his or her successes and being "bombarded." Then a third person will be the target, and so on.*

Circulate and assist the groups, as needed. Although the students are expected to enjoy the exercise, make sure that they appreciate its seriousness and do not engage in any kind of teasing or put-downs. If you observe any student using the third person ("She is industrious and energetic.") when labeling a "target," stop the person and help him or her rephrase the statement in the second person. ("You are industrious and energetic.") Lead a follow-up discussion.

Discussion Questions:
1. How do you feel after doing this exercise?
2. What did you learn about yourself? ...about other members of your group?
3. How did you decide which accomplishments to include on your list?
4. Why do you suppose we spend so much time thinking about our failures and deficiencies when we have all accomplished so much?
5. Where can you put your target so that it will continue to remind you of your successes?

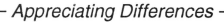

Success Inventory
Experience Sheet

Your life is full of successes, one after another, year after year. The things you've accomplished could fill a book. Look back now at the child you were and the young adult you have become. Recall some of the many things you've learned and achieved, and write the most memorable here:

• Five skills I mastered before the age of 5 were:

1. _____

2. _____

3. _____

4. _____

5. _____

• Four things I accomplished between the ages of 5 and 8 were:

1. _____

2. _____

3. _____

4. _____

• Four of my achievements between the ages of 8 and 11 were:

1. _____

2. _____

3. _____

4. _____

• Five major things I've accomplished between the ages of 11 and now are:

1. _____

2. _____

3. _____

4. _____

5. _____

TARGET
Worksheet

A Time I Felt Important
A Circle Session

Objectives:
The students will:
—recognize and describe their own importance.
—identify strengths, talents, and special abilities in themselves and others.
—practice methods of positive self-talk.

Introduce the Topic:
We are worthwhile just because we are alive. Every person is. But for some strange reason, we often put ourselves and others down. We tell ourselves that we are not adequate, not worthwhile, not important. Today, we're going to do just the opposite. Our topic for this session is, "A Time I Felt Important."

Can you recall a time when you were very aware that you were an important, worthwhile person? Maybe you felt important because someone else was looking to you for advice and direction. Or maybe you were being honored for an achievement. Perhaps you made the winning touchdown, run, basket, or goal. Have you ever been selected to represent your class or school at some event? Have you ever been looked up to by the younger kids in your neighborhood? Just once, did you really believe it when your parent told you how important you are to the family? Think about it for a few moments. The topic is, "A Time I Felt Important."

Discussion Questions:
1. What similarities were there in the kinds of things we were doing when we felt important?
2. How much do other people influence our feelings about ourselves?
3. To what degree do others have to recognize our importance before we see it in ourselves?
4. What can you do to help a friend, a parent, or a younger brother or sister feel important?

A Time I Stood Up for Something I Strongly Believe In
A Circle Session

Objectives:

The students will:

—describe times when they behaved assertively regarding a strongly held value or principle.

—demonstrate an understanding of assertive versus nonassertive behaviors.

Introduce the Topic:

Many times during our lives, we are given the opportunity to speak out for the things we believe in. By now, most of us have experienced at least one such occasion. Taking a stand can be a difficult experience, especially if friends or relatives don't agree with our position. Even when they do agree, it's not necessarily easy to state our beliefs publicly. Today, we're going to talk about the conviction and determination these situations demand. Our topic is, "I Stood Up for Something I Strongly Believe In."

Perhaps you saw a group of people doing something that you felt was wrong, and decided that they needed to be confronted. Maybe you observed some kids teasing or harassing another kid, and intervened. Or maybe, during a conversation about a controversial subject, you stated your beliefs even though everyone else in the group held the opposing view. Perhaps you decided to leave a group that had started using drugs, but before you left made sure that everyone knew you thought what they were doing was wrong and dangerous. One thing is generally true. When we stand up for what we believe in, we feel a sense of pride and accomplishment, and the more often we do it, the greater our courage the next time it happens. If you decide to share, please don't mention the names of the other people involved. The topic is, "I Stood Up for Something I Strongly Believe In."

Discussion Questions:

1. As you look back on the situation you shared, how do you feel about it right now?
2. Why is it sometimes hard to stand up for your beliefs?
3. What are the risks of taking a stand? What are the benefits?
4. What are some ills in our society that people need to take a stand against?

I Was Labeled Based on Something I Couldn't Change
A Circle Session

Objectives:
The students will:
—describe a time when they were stereotyped by labeling language, and how they responded.
—identify ways to discourage the practice of labeling.

Introduce the Topic:

One of the problems with labels — even flattering labels — is that they limit people. They cause us to see the labeled person as whatever the label says, rather than as a complex, unique individual. Today, we're going to talk about our own experiences with being labeled, and how those labels caused us to feel and react. Our topic is, "I Was Labeled Based on Something I Couldn't Change." Think of a time when someone, or a group of people, labeled you. Maybe the label had to do with your appearance, your athletic ability — or lack of it — or your way of talking. Perhaps you were labeled based on your racial, ethnic, or religious background, or something that another member of your family did. People get stuck with labels based on problem complexions, hair color, height, weight, facial features — even the size of their feet. We label people for their abilities and their disabilities, and we even label people for something that happened years ago. Think of a label that you're dealing with now or one that you carried in the past. Tell us how you feel about that label and the effect it has had on your life. Think about it for a few moments. The topic is, "I Was Labeled Based on Something I Couldn't Change."

Discussion Questions:
1. How did most of us react to being labeled?
2. Why do we label people? What purpose does it serve?
3. What can you do to discourage your peers from labeling one another?
4. What can you do to influence adults who thoughtlessly or maliciously use labels?

Something I Can Do to Promote Peace and Understanding
A Circle Session

Objectives:
The students will:
—identify ways in which they can contribute to world peace.
—describe world events that have promoted global peace.

Introduce the Topic:
Today in our circle, we're going to talk about people getting along. Our topic is, "Something I Can Do to Promote Peace and Understanding."

What can you do as a student and a citizen to make our school, community, and world a more peaceful place? Maybe you can join an organization that works for social justice, or write letters to members of congress asking them to do more to promote equal opportunity for all citizens. Reading the newspaper so that you know what's going on is a good place to start. Promoting inclusion and interdependence at home, at school, and in your neighborhood contributes to understanding and peace, too. Does your church or synagogue have activities that promote understanding? Think about it for a few moments and tell us about a way that you can make a difference. The topic is, "Something I Can Do to Promote Peace and Understanding."

Discussion Questions:
1. How do you feel when you do something that helps others?
2. Why is it important to help other people?
3. Some very important things have happened in the last few years that have given us more peace in the world. What are they?
4. How can we ensure that peace and understanding among people keep growing?

Language as Pilot
A Communications Experiment

Objectives:
The students will:
—practice communicating clearly and accurately.
—describe problems caused by imprecise communication and
  differing interpretations.
—describe how they manage their behavior to achieve
  success when sightless.

Materials:
desks, tables, crumpled paper, and other objects generally
available in the classroom

Directions:
   Begin by telling the students that you would like them to
cooperate in conducting an experiment that relates to language
and communication. Without any further explanation, ask the
students to help you build a runway. Construct the runway out
of furniture and people. Make it about 15 to 20 feet long and
wide enough for a person to walk down. Next, litter the runway
with debris, books, papers, pencils, and other small objects
which will not cause a blindfolded person to trip or fall.

   When the runway is ready, ask a student volunteer to role
play the pilot of an airplane landing on the runway. Then ask a
volunteer to play the part of the air-traffic controller trying to help
the pilot land the plane by giving directions over an imaginary
radio transmitter. As soon as two students volunteer, ask them
to move to opposite ends of the runway.

   Blindfold the pilot. Explain that a storm has hit and lightning
has knocked out the transmitter of the plane. The receiver is
still working so the pilot can get messages, but can't send them.
Indicate that the storm has created havoc on the runway. Debris is all over the place. The control tower must try to land the
plane without damage by sending directions over the radio. The

visibility is zero, so the pilot must rely only on these messages for a safe landing. If the pilot brushes against any of the objects on the runway, the plane is considered crashed.

Allow several teams of pilots and controllers to attempt to land the plane safely. After each attempt, briefly discuss the problems each team encountered. Then ask the students to put the classroom back in order and return to their seats for a general discussion.

Discussion Questions:
1. How did you feel when you were the pilot?
2. How did you compensate for being sightless?
3. How did you feel when you were the controller?
4. What specifically did you do to become your pilot's "eyes?"
5. How can we communicate clear and exact messages?
6. Has anything like this ever happened to you? Tell us about a time when you had trouble getting a precise message across or correctly understanding someone else's message.
7. What have you learned about language and communication from this experiment?
8. What did this experience teach you about functioning effectively with a disability? ...about working cooperatively with someone who has a disability?

Common Communication Blocks
Role-Play and Discussion

Objectives:
The students will:
—demonstrate common ways of responding to another person that may block communication.
—describe how different ways of responding may affect a speaker.
—discuss what constitutes effective and ineffective communication

Materials:
one copy of the experience sheet, "Communication Blockers" for each student; chalkboard and chalk or chart paper and markers

Directions:
Write the following list on the board or chart paper for the students to see when they enter class:
- Interrupting
- Challenging/Accusing/Contradicting
- Dominating
- Judging
- Advising
- Interpreting
- Probing
- Criticizing/Name-calling/Put-downs

Begin the activity by asking the students to think of a heading or title for the list on the board. Write their suggestions down and discuss each one briefly. Add the suggested title, "Communication Stoppers," and ask the students if they can imagine how these behaviors might have the effect of hampering communication — or stopping it altogether.

Ask the students to help you role-play each behavior to see what kind of effect it does have on communication. Invite a volunteer to start a conversation with you. Explain that he or she may talk bout anything that comes to mind, and should attempt to continue the conversation as long as possible, or until you call time.

As the student begins to speak, respond with one of the communication stoppers from the list. Use appropriate gestures, volume, and tone, and make your response as convincing as possible. Continue using examples of that particular communication stopper until (1) the student gives up talking, or (2) the point has been sufficiently made.

After each demonstration, lead a class discussion about the effects of that communication behavior. Ask the discussion questions listed at the end of these directions, and others suggested by the demonstration. *The following elaboration on the communication stoppers includes suggestions for conducting each demonstration, as well as important points to make during discussion.* (Distribute the experience sheets at the end of the activity. Suggest that the students keep them in their notebooks and refer to them occasionally.)

Interrupting

Demonstration: Butt in time and again as the student talks, with statements about yourself and things that have happened to you. For example, if the student says, "I have a friend named Sue, and...," interrupt with, "Oh, I know her—well, a little. We met the other day when...etc., etc."

Discussion: Point out how frustrating it is to be interrupted, and how futile it is to continue a conversation when interruptions occur over and over. Interrupting is probably the most common way in which communication is stopped.

Advising

Demonstration: Give lots of unasked-for advice. Use statements like, "Well, if I were you...," "I think you should...," and "Have you tried..." If the student says, "I have a friend named Sue, and...," respond with, "Sue has a lot of problems. Take my advice and steer clear or her." or "Be careful what you say. Sue can't keep a secret for three minutes." Etc.

Discussion: By giving unsolicited advice, a person immediately assumes a position of superiority. Advice-giving says, "I know better than you do." Advice may also cause the speaker to feel powerless to control his or her own life.

Judging

Demonstration: Evaluate the student and everything he or she says. For example, if the student says, "I have a friend named Sue, and...," say, "Yeah, Sue's part of that stuck-up snob crowd." If the student says, "I want to see that new De Niro movie." say, "Don't waste your money, it's lousy."

Discussion: Judging retards communication even when the judgment is positive. Not only does the "judge" assume a superior position, his or her evaluations may so completely contradict the speaker's own feelings that a contest or argument ensues—or further communication is pointless.

Interpreting

Demonstration: Analyze everything the student says in order to reveal its "deeper meaning." If the student says, "I have a friend named Sue, and...," say, "You think having Sue as a friend will improve your popularity." If the student denies the desire to be popular, say, "That's because you don't have a good self-image."

Discussion: Interpreting and analyzing say that the listener is unwilling to accept the speaker (or the speaker's statements) at face value. Not to mention that the interpretation is frequently wrong.

Dominating

Demonstration: Take over the conversation. If the student says, "I have a friend named Sue, and...," jump in with, "I know Sue's brother. He is..., and not only that, he..., and so..., because..., blah, blah, blah, etc., etc., ad nauseam.

Discussion: We all know how frustrating and annoying it is to be in a conversation with someone who always has something better and more interesting to say than we do. In addition, when one person dominates a conversation, others are forced to use another communication stopper, *interrupting*, just to get a word in.

Probing

Demonstration: Ask question after question in a demanding tone. If the student says, "I have a friend named Sue, and...," ask, "Why do you hang out with her?" As soon as the student begins to answer, ask, "How long have you known her?" "Is her hair naturally blonde?" And so on.

Discussion: Probing tends to put the speaker on the defensive by asking him or her to justify or explain every statement. More importantly, questions may lead the speaker away from what she or he originally wanted to say. The questioner thus controls the conversation *and* its direction.

Continued, next page

Challenging/Accusing/Contradicting

Demonstration: Contradict what the student says and accuse him or her of being wrong. For example, if the student says, "I have a friend named Sue, and...," say, "She's not really your friend. You know her because she's Anna's friend." If the student says, "Sue and I have a lot in common." say, "You're dreaming. Name one thing!"

Discussion: Contradictions and accusations put the speaker on the spot, and make it necessary for her or him to take a defensive position. They also say to the speaker, "You are wrong." or "You are bad."

Criticizing/Name-calling/Putting-down

Demonstration: Make sarcastic, negative remarks in response to everything the student says. If the student says, "I have a friend named Sue, and...," say, "You jerk, what are you hanging out with her for." If the student says, "Because I like her..." respond, "You never did have good sense."

Discussion: Criticism diminishes the speaker. Few of us want to continue a conversation in which we are being diminished. Name-calling and put-downs are frequently veiled in humor, but may nonetheless be hurtful and damaging to a relationship.

Discussion Questions:

1. How did you (the speaker) feel?
2. What effect does this type of response have on the speaker? ...on the conversation? ...on the relationship?
3. Has this ever happened to you? What did you say and/or do?
4. Under what circumstances would it be okay to respond like this?

Communication Blockers
Experience Sheet

**Have you ever tried to have a conversation with some-
one who wouldn't let you finish a sentence? Have you ever
tried to discuss a problem with someone who had an answer for everything? Bad communication habits can stop a
conversation short. Here are a few to avoid:**

Interrupting

Interruptions are the most common cause of blocked communication. No one likes to be interrupted in the middle of a
sentence. When interruptions happen over and over again,
you may begin to feel as though talking is a waste of time.

Advising

Few people enjoy getting advice they didn't ask for. Statements that begin with, "Well, if I were you...," or "If you ask
me...," are like red flags. Advice-giving says, "I'm superior. I
know better than you do." Advice can also cause a person
to feel helpless — as though he can't make a good decision
on his own.

Judging

When you tell people that their ideas or feelings are wrong,
you are suggesting that you know more than they do. If your
ideas are drastically different from theirs, they'll either defend
themselves (argue) or give up on the conversation. Even
positive judgments like, "You're the smartest student in
class," don't work if the person you're talking to doesn't *feel*
very smart.

Interpreting

Some people develop a habit of analyzing everything (including statements) to reveal "deeper meanings." When you
interpret or analyze, you imply an unwillingness to accept the
speaker or the speaker's statements just as they are. Analyzing is for psychiatrists and counselors, and a lot of the
time even *they* are wrong!

Dominating

We all know how frustrating and annoying it is to be in a conversation with someone who always has something better and more interesting to say than we do. In addition, when you dominate a conversation, others are forced to use another communication stopper, *interrupting*, just to get a word in.

Probing

Asking a lot of questions ("Why did you go there?" "Who did you see?" "What did he do?") tends to put the speaker on the defensive by requiring her to explain every statement. More importantly, your questions may lead the speaker *away from* what she originally wanted to say. If you ask too many questions, you are controlling, not sharing, the conversation.

Challenging/Accusing/Contradicting

Have you ever tried to talk with someone who challenged everything you said, insisted that your ideas were wrong, or said that what happened was your fault? Contradictions and accusations put the speaker on the spot, and make the speaker defensive.

Criticizing/Name-calling/Put-downs

Don't make sarcastic or negative remarks in response to the things someone says. Criticism whittles away at self-esteem. Hardly anyone wants to continue a conversation that's making him feel bad or small. Even name-calling and put-downs that sound funny can still be hurtful. In the long run, they damage friendships.

Play It Back!
Dyad Sequence and Discussion

Objectives:
The students will:
—demonstrate attentive listening with a series of partners.
—explain how they let others know they are listening.

Materials:
chalkboard and chalk

Directions:
Assign the students to groups of eight or ten. (An even number in each group is essential for this activity to work. If a group is one short, join that group during the activity.)

Ask the students to choose a partner. Explain that both people will take turns speaking to the same topic. As the first person (**A**) speaks for 1 minute, the second person (**B**) must listen very carefully, gathering information very much like a tape recorder. The listener should not interrupt or ask questions, except for clarification. When time is called, **B** will have 1 minute to "play back" to **A** as accurately as possible what he or she heard. Then **A** and **B** will switch roles. **B** will become the speaker and talk about the same topic for 1 minute while **A** listens. Then **A** will have 1 minute to "play back" what she or he heard. This will complete the first round, and the students will find new partners within their group.

Signal the end of each minute and give clear instructions. Conduct enough rounds so that every person is paired once with every other person in his or her group. (For example, if groups contain eight students, conduct seven rounds.)

Continued, next page

Suggested Topics:
"My Favorite Hobby or Pastime"
"My Favorite Food"
"My Favorite TV Show or Movie"
"My Favorite Story, Poem, Book, or Magazine"
"My Favorite Animal"
"My Favorite Game or Sport"
"My Favorite Song or Musical Group"
"Something That Makes Me Happy"
"Something I Want To Do This Weekend"
"Something I'm Looking Forward To"

Discussion Questions:
1. How did you feel as the speaker during this exercise?
2. How did you feel as the listener?
3. What was hardest about listening like a tape recorder?
4. Did speaking and/or listening get harder or easier as you went from partner to partner?
5. How does silent, attentive listening lead to effective communication? Why is it a good idea to "play back" what you hear?
6. What are some things you can do to show someone that you are really listening?
7. How can you let someone know that you are listening if he or she has a vision loss? ...a hearing loss?

The Active Listener
Communication Skill Practice

Objectives:
The students will:
—define the role of the receiver in communication.
—identify and demonstrate "active listening" behaviors.

Materials:
a diagrammatic model of the communications process (see below) drawn on the chalkboard or chart paper; a list of topics written on the chalkboard (see below); one copy of the experience sheet, "Be an Active Listener!" for each student

Directions:
On the chalkboard and chart paper, draw a simple diagram illustrating the communication process. For example, print the words, **SENDER** and **RECEIVER** and draw two arrows — one going in each direction — between the two words.

Explain to the students that in order for two people to enjoy and encourage each other, to work, play, or solve problems together, they need to be able to communicate effectively. In your own words, say: *In every example of communication, no matter how small, a message is sent from one person (the sender) to the other person (the receiver). The message is supposed to tell the receiver something about the feelings and/or thoughts of the sender. Because the sender cannot "give" the receiver his or her feelings and thoughts, they have to be "coded" in words. Good communicators pick words that describe their feelings and thoughts as closely as possible. Nonverbal "signals" almost always accompany the verbal message; for example, a smile, a frown, or a hand gesture. Some-*

times the entire message is nonverbal. Good communicators send nonverbal signals that exactly match their feelings and thoughts.

Ask the students to describe what a good receiver says and does to show that s/he is interested in what the sender is saying and is really listening. Write their ideas on the chalkboard. Be sure to include these behaviors:

1. Face the sender.

2. Look into the sender's eyes.

3. Be relaxed, but attentive.

4. Listen to the words and try to picture in your own mind what the sender is telling you.

5. Don't interrupt or fidget. When it is your turn to respond, don't change the subject or start telling your own story.

6. If you don't understand something, wait for the sender to pause and then ask, "What do you mean by..."

7. Try to feel what the sender is feeling (show empathy).

8. Respond in ways that let the sender know that you are listening and understand what is being said. Ways of responding might include nodding, saying "uh huh," or giving feedback that proves you are listening, for example:

   • **Briefly summarize**: "You're saying that you might have to quit the team in order to have time for a paper route."

   • **Restate feelings**: "You must be feeling pretty bad." or "You sound really happy!"

Tell the students that this type of listening is called *active listening*. Ask them if they can explain why the word *active* is used to describe it.

Ask the students to form groups of three. Tell them to decide who is **A**, who is **B**, and who is **C**. Announce that you are going to give the students an opportunity to practice active listening. Explain the process: *In the first round, **A** will be the sender and **B** will be the receiver and will use active listening. **C** will be the observer. **C's** job is to notice how well **B** listens, and report his/her observations at the end of the round. I will be the timekeeper. We will have three rounds, so that you can each have a turn in all three roles. When you are the sender, pick a topic from the list on the board, and remember to pause occasionally so that your partner can respond.*

Signal the start of the first round. Call time after 3 minutes. Have the observers give feedback for 1 minute. Tell the students to switch roles. Conduct two more rounds. Lead a follow-up discussion. Distribute the experience sheet and suggest that the students keep it in their notebooks and refer to it from time to time.

Discussion Questions:
1. How did it feel to "active listen?"
2. What was it like to be the observer?
3. When you were the sender, how did you feel having someone really listen to you?
4. What was easiest about active listening? What was hardest?
5. What did you learn from your observer?
6. Why is it important to learn to be a good listener?

List of topics:
"A Time I Needed Some Help"
"Something I'd Like to Do Better"
"A Problem I Need to Solve"
"A Time I Got Into an Argument"
"A Time I Had to Make a Tough Decision"
"Something I'd Like to Be or Do When I'm an Adult"

Be an Active Listener!
Experience Sheet

Listening is a vert important part of good communication. Listed below are characteristics of a good listener. Check (✔) the ones that describe you most of the time.

A good listener:

___ Faces the speaker.

___ Looks into the speaker's eyes.

___ Is relaxed, but attentive.

___ keeps an open mind.

___ Listens to the words and tries to picture what the speaker is saying.

___ Doesn't interrupt or fidget.

___ Waits for the sender to pause before asking questions.

___ Tries to feel what the sender is feeling (shows empathy).

___ Nods and says "uh huh," or summarizes to let the speaker know he/she is listening.

What is your strongest quality as a listener?_____

_____

What is your weakest quality as a listener? _____

_____

How can you become a better listener? _____

_____

The I's Have It!
Experience Sheet and Discussion

Objectives:
The students will:
—compare "I" messages and "you" messages and describe their differences.
—identify the three parts of an "I" message.
—practice formulating "I" messages.

Materials:
one copy of the experience sheet, "Don't Say 'You' — Say 'I'" for each student; chalkboard and chalk or chart paper and magic marker; diagram of the communications model (see the activity, "The Active Receiver") on the board or chart

Directions:
Review the communications model used in the activity, "The Active Receiver." Ask the students to summarize the roles of the sender and receiver. Then in your own words, explain to the students:

When you are the sender, one of the most powerful messages you can send — especially if you are having a problem or conflict with the receiver is an "I" message. An "I" message tells the receiver what the problem is, how you feel about it, and what you want (or don't want) the receiver to do. Many times, we send "you" messages when we would be much better off sending "I" messages. "You" messages are often blaming and threatening, frequently make the receiver feel mad or hurt, usually make the problem worse, and many times don't even describe the problem. "You" messages can even <u>start</u> a conflict where none existed before.

Extemporaneously demonstrate with one or two of your students. For example, say:

Continued, next page

Rodney, you are fooling around again. If you don't get busy and finish that assignment, the whole group will have to stay in during the break, and it will be your fault!

vs.

Rodney, I'm worried that this assignment won't be finished by the break. I'd like to see you concentrate much harder on your work.

Anna, are you forgetful or just lazy? Look at all those open marking pens. You ruined them!

vs.

Anna, I get very discouraged when I see that the marking pens have been left open all night, because they dry out, and then we can't use them anymore. I want you to help me by remembering to cover them.

Distribute the experience sheets. Go over the directions with the students. Allow a few minutes for the students to individually complete the experience sheet.

Take one cartoon at a time, and ask two volunteers to demonstrate first the "you" message, and then their own "I" messages. Invite other members of the class to come forward, step into the role play, and substitute their own "I" message. Contrast the various efforts and discuss their effectiveness.

Discussion Questions:

1. What is the hardest part of composing an "I" message?
2. How do you feel when someone gives you a "you" message? ...an "I" message?
3. How can using "I" messages help us settle arguments and resolve conflicts?

Don't Say "You" — Say "I"
Experience Sheet

Good Communication is the Key!

When another person does something we don't like, we may be tempted to send the person a **"you" message**. "You" messages get their name from the fact that they often start with the word "you." They are blaming messages. They can make the other person feel mad or hurt — and they can make the situation worse.

Try using an **"I" message** instead. "I" messages talk about your feelings and needs. They can help the other person understand you. Here's how to make an "I" message:

1. **Describe the situation.** It may help to begin with the words, "When..." or "When you..."

2. **Say how you feel.**
   "When you......................, I feel.."

3. **Describe what you want the person to do.**
   "When you................., I feel..,
   and I want you to..."

Now, you try it! Read the "you" message in the first cartoon bubble. Then write a better message—an "I" message—in the second bubble.

Cindy, this phone does not belong to you! If you don't hang up right now, I'm going to tell Mom. You're such a selfish hog!

"You" Message

"I" Message

When you _____,
I feel _____,
and I want you to _____
_____

All the other kids are going to the party! It's not fair that you make me stay home an baby-sit all the time. You're ruining my life!

"You" Message

"I" Message

When you _____,
I feel _____,
_____
and I want _____
_____
_____.

Follow My Lead
Group Experiment and Discussion

Objectives:

The students will:

—use precise verbal and nonverbal communication to lead a partner to a hidden object.

—describe the importance of precise communication.

Materials:

a large open area, as free as possible of physical obstacles; scarves, large handkerchiefs, or strips of opaque fabric to use as blindfolds

Directions:

Note: You may wish to conduct the second round of this activity in a series of three to five 3-minute segments. This will limit the number of pairs on the floor at any given time, diminishing sound interference and increasing safety.

Begin the activity by talking briefly about the need for clarity, accuracy, and conciseness in communication. Announce that the students are going to participate in an activity that will test their ability to communicate with clarity.

Have the students choose partners and decide who will be the Leader in the first round. Then, in your own words, explain: *When you are the Leader, you are going to use clear, precise verbal communication to guide your partner, who will be blindfolded, to an object hidden somewhere in the room. You must use as few directions as possible, so pick your words carefully. Stay close to your partner, talking quietly by distinctly, but DO NOT touch your partner. Blindfolded partners may ask questions for clarification. Remember that other pairs will be moving about the room, and it is your responsibility as the leader to prevent collisions. At the end of 3 minutes, I'll call time and you will switch roles for the second round.*

Continued, next page

Together, have each pair pick an object (book, key, pen, backpack, etc.) to be "found" during the activity. Instruct the Leaders to blindfold their partners. Then give the Leaders 1 minute to hide their object somewhere in the room.

Allow about 3 minutes for the Leaders to guide their partners to the hidden objects. Then gather the class together and give these instructions for the second round: *The goal of the Leader is the same in the second round — to lead your blindfolded partner to a hidden object. However, you must do the guiding nonverbally. You MAY NOT touch your partner, but you will have 2 minutes before the round to agree on a series of signals for various movements, such as Left, Right, Stop, Up, Down, etc. You may use claps, snaps, stomps, taps or any other clear signal that you can invent. Blindfolded partners may ask questions for clarification; however, Leaders may not answer in words.*

Have the partners pick a second object. Allow 2 minutes for signal planning. Then have the Leaders blindfold their partners and hide the object. Allow 3 minutes for the Leaders to guide their partner to the object. Conclude the activity with a class discussion.

Discussion Questions:
1. What was it like to be the Leader in round one? ...in round two?
2. How did you feel when you were the partner with a vision loss?
3. How successfully did you communicate as a Leader?
4. What were some of the problems you encountered and how did you solve them?
5. What did you learn about communication from this activity?
6. What did you learn about leadership?

A Time I Listened Well
A Circle Session

Objectives:
The students will:
—describe a time when they listened effectively.
—identify effective listening behaviors.

Introduce the Topic:
Most of us appreciate having someone really listen to us. In this session we are going to turn this idea around and talk about how it feels to listen to someone else. The topic is, "A Time I Listened Well."

Can you remember a time when you really paid attention to someone and listened carefully to what he or she said. This means that you didn't interrupt with your own ideas or daydream about your own plans, but really concentrated and tried to understand what the other person was attempting to get across. Maybe you've listened to a friend like that, or a younger brother or sister, or a teacher or coach. Think about it for a few moments and, if you wish, tell us about, "A Time I Listened Well."

Discussion Questions:
1. What kinds of things make listening difficult?
2. Why is it important to listen to others?
3. What could you do to improve your listening?
4. How do you feel when someone really listens to you?

What I Think Good Communication Is
A Circle Session

Objectives:
The students will:
—identify specific components of effective communication.
—state specific reasons why good communication is important.

Introduce the Topic:
Today's topic for discussion is, "What I Think Good Communication Is". Communication is an exchange of thoughts, feelings, opinions, or information between two or more people. Today we're going to focus on the ingredients of good communication. There are no right or wrong answers; whatever you contribute will help us develop a better understanding of what's involved. If you like, try thinking about a person with whom you've had success communicating and tell us some of the things that happen during your interactions with that person. Take a few minutes, and then we'll begin sharing on our topic, "What I Think Good Communication Is."

Discussion Questions:
1. What quality or ingredient of good communication was mentioned most often during our sharing?
2. Why is it important to practice good communication?

I Like My Friend Who...
A Friendship Game

Objective:
The students will:
—become better acquainted with one another.
—experience a sense of inclusion in the group.

Materials:
chairs arranged in a large circle

Directions:
Have the students sit in a large circle. Begin the game yourself by standing in the center of the circle. Explain that you are going to call out categories into which one or more students fit. When a category is named, students who fit that category are to stand in place and then sit down before the next category is called.

Take the first few turns, each time calling out, "I Like My Friend Who..." and finishing the sentence with a different category. As soon as the students grasp the idea, choose someone else to be the leader while you take a seat in the circle. Continue changing leaders after every few calls.

The possibilities for categories are endless. Here are a few suggestions:
...knows how to do a flip.
...is wearing white socks.
...has brown eyes.
...likes to swim.
...has a baby brother or sister.
...has flown in an airplane.
...likes spinach.
...has a cat at home.
...was born in another country.
...plays a musical instrument.
...speaks more than one language.

Continued, next page

After several categories are named and players have stood up and down many times, proceed to the more active part of the game. Announce that when the leader calls out a category, players who fit the category must quickly change seats. Explain that the leader must try to grab one of the seats vacated by a player, which will leave someone else without a chair. That person becomes the new leader, stands in the middle, and calls out the next category.

Allow the game to continue until everyone is energized, stopping it before the students run out of categories or become bored.

The Friendship Shake
Introductions and Conversation Starters

Objectives:
The students will:
—practice making introductions.
—practice starting and maintaining conversations.

Materials:
one copy of the experience sheet, "Conversation Log" for each student; chalkboard and chalk

Directions:
Announce that today the group is going practice important friendship skills: making introductions and starting conversations. Point out that if people don't know how to make introductions or begin conversations, many opportunities to start new friendships are lost. It's not uncommon to feel a desire to know someone, yet be unsure where or how to begin.

Use the "Handshake" game to form three groups of students: Ask the students to "meditate" for a moment and SILENTLY decide on a number — one, two, or three. Then direct the students to get up and SILENTLY find their numerical "soulmates," by mingling around and shaking hands with one another. If their number is one, they are to firmly shake each hand one time. If their number is two, they firmly shake each hand twice. If their number is three, they shake three times. Explain that when two students with different numbers shake hands, they will experience a moment of tension when one stops shaking and the other continues. But when both have the same number, they will stop shaking at the same moment and will *know* instantly that they are in the same group. They must then stick together while searching for other members of their group. (The resulting groups will probably be about the same size, but don't be concerned if they're not.)

Continued, next page

Introducing Oneself

Once the groups are formed, get everyone's attention and offer the following model for introducing oneself to another person:

1. Approach the person you want to meet.
2. Say, "Hello," "Hi," or offer some other greeting.
3. Say, "My name is..."
4. Wait for the person to say his or her name *or* ask, "What's your name?"

All together, the steps sound like this: "Hi, my name's Diana. What's your name?"

Introducing Others

Give the students a few minutes to practice these steps with one another in their newly formed groups. Then offer this model for introducing two people to each other:

1. Look at the first person and say that person's name.
2. Tell the first person the second person's name
3. Repeat the process with the second person.

All together, the steps sound like this: "Andy, this is Lucy Becerra. Lucy, this is Andy Gilbert."

Have the students practice the steps in their groups, experiencing several rounds of introductions with different members. Then point out that a conversation frequently follows an introduction.

Starting a Conversation

The following steps are helpful when starting a conversation with another person:

1. Look at the person with whom you want to speak.
2. Say something about yourself (for example, something you like).
3. Ask the person about something he or she likes.
4. Offer a positive response related to what the person says.

All together, the steps sound like this:

Person 1: "I really enjoy gymnastics and bicycling. What do you like to do?"

Person 2: "I like bicycling too, but I'm not sure where the good bike paths are around here."

Person 1: "I know some great bike paths. Why don't we go bicycling together some Sunday?"

Have the students pair up within their groups and practice starting conversations. Remind them to switch partners every few minutes. After the students have practiced for 5 to 10 minutes, reconvene the class and distribute the "Conversation Log" experience sheets. Explain that you want them to keep track of conversations they initiate over the next week, making notes on their log. Answer any questions. Conclude the activity with a class discussion.

Discussion Questions:

1. How did you feel when you were introducing yourself? ...when you were introducing two other people?
2. How did you feel when you were attempting to start a conversation?
3. What is the easiest part of starting a conversation? What is the hardest part?
4. What are some other methods of getting to know new people?
5. How do you feel when the person you want to talk with doesn't seem interested? What's the best thing to do in instances like that?

Follow-up: Approximately 1 week following this activity, have the students get back together in their "soulmate" groups and share highlights from their Conversation Logs.

Conversation Log
Experience Sheet

For one week, notice each time you <u>make an introduction or start a conversation</u>. Pay attention to what happens and how you feel. Use the chart below to record your observations, feelings, and thoughts.

Day	I Talked With	What I Think/Feel
1		
2		
3		
4		
5		
6		
7		

Two Sides of Friendship
Small-Group Graphics and Discussion

Objectives:
The students will:
—define friendship in their own terms.
—graphically represent effective and ineffective friendship behaviors.

Materials:
three or more large pieces of butcher paper; masking tape; marking pens in assorted colors

Directions:
Use the "Handshake" game to divide the class into three groups (see the activity, "The Friendship Shake").

Give a large piece of butcher paper and several markers to each group. Have each group select two members to start the activity. Explain: *One person lies down on the paper, assuming any position he or she wishes, and the other traces around that person's body with a marking pen to make a "person shape." When the two are finished, they turn the paper over and hand their markers to two other members of the group, who repeat the process using the reverse side of the paper.*

Have the groups tape their drawings to different walls around the room. Explain that as a group, you want them to brainstorm qualities that they value in a friend. These might include *honesty, loyalty, good listening skills, willingness to be there for you, friendliness, affection, helpfulness*, and so forth. When a student has an idea, he or she must pick up a marking pen, go up to the drawing, and write the idea inside the person outline. At the same time, the student is to explain the idea to the rest of the group. Encourage all group members to get involved.

Continued, next page

Circulate and stimulate discussion within each group. Get the students to focus on the values they are expressing. For example, say: *Cindy, you mentioned that you value "being friendly." Would you please explain what that means to you? Jack, you and Lu both said friends are always honest. How do you feel if a friend lies to you?*

When the groups have finished filling in their person shapes, have them turn the paper over and use the other side to record qualities they *do not* value in a friend. These might include *lying, tattling, backbiting, pressuring, name-calling, put downs,* and so forth. Encourage them to think of their own experiences, and fill up the drawing with ideas.

Have each group share its completed drawing (front and back) with the entire class. Facilitate discussion.

Discussion Questions:
1. Which values came up in all three groups?
2. What ideas did you get from any of the drawings that you hadn't considered before? What are your thoughts about those ideas?
3. How will you use learnings from this activity in your own friendships?

Setting Friendship Goals
Experience Sheet and Dyad Sharing

Objectives:
The students will:
—identify what they and others like and don't like about their own friendship behaviors.
—identify ways to decrease negative friendship behaviors and increase positive ones.
—formulate a goal and plan for improving one friendship behavior.

Materials:
one copy of the experience sheet, "Becoming a Better Friend" for each student; chalkboard or chart paper

Directions:
Begin by reminding the students of previous discussions/assignments concerning friendship. Announce that today the students are going to concentrate on evaluating their own friendship behaviors.

Ask several volunteers to name things they could begin doing (or stop doing) that would make them a better friend. List ideas on the board, such as:
* Learn how to start a conversation with a new person.
* Volunteer to help someone study for a test.
* Reach out to someone of a different race or cultural background.
* Include someone with a disability in your activities.
* Invite someone to eat lunch with you.
* Help a friend learn a new skill or game.
* Stick up for your friends (be loyal).
* Learn how to settle conflicts and negotiate differences.
* Practice giving compliments.
* Smile and use good eye contact when talking with others.
* Bring together friends from different groups in some common pursuit.

Continued, next page

Ask the students to name some behaviors that others respond to positively and negatively. Offer examples from your own experience. You might say: *My positive friendship behaviors are that I always do what I say I'm going to do. In addition, I have a positive attitude. I smile a lot, and I try to remember to tell people when I like something they've done. A negative behavior I need to work on is letting my thoughts jump ahead during conversations, which sometimes leads me to interrupt the person who is speaking.*

Continue taking examples from the group until you think the students have the idea. Then, distribute the experience sheet. Go over it briefly, answering any questions. Allow the students approximately 10 to 15 minutes to complete the sheet.

Have the students pair up. Instruct the partners to each share three positive behaviors and one negative behavior, as you did in your earlier example. Allow about 5 minutes for sharing, signaling the partners at the halfway point.

Get the attention of the pairs, and take a few moments to talk about the importance of goals. Point out that no one is born knowing how to make and keep friends; rather, these behaviors are learned. When behaviors are learned, they can also be changed. Change involves setting goals for new behaviors and implementing step-by-step plans for achieving those goals. Give the partners an additional 5 to 10 minutes to share their goals and action plans. Suggest that they help each other formulate steps for achieving their goals. Lead a culminating class discussion.

Discussion Questions:
1. How do you explain the fact that some people have so many friends and others have few?
2. Why are friendships important? What do we gain from having friends?
3. What kinds of help and support do you need to reach your friendship goal? How and from whom will you get that help and support?

Becoming a Better Friend
Experience Sheet

Friends are important! If you could take three people with you on a trip around the world, whom would you take? Why?

Name	Reason
1. _____	_____
2. _____	_____
3. _____	_____

How can you keep it growing? Do you have a friendship with someone that just keeps getting better? What have you done to keep it growing?

_____

_____

What do you value in your friends?
Complete this statement: *People can show their friendship to me by...*

_____

_____

Name at least four of *your own* friendship behaviors that others seem to like:

1. _____ 3. _____

2. _____ 4. _____

Name two of *your own* friendship behaviors that seem to turn others off:

1. _____

2. _____

Think of *one way* in which you would like to improve your friendship behavior. Write a GOAL here:

_____

_____

_____

To achieve your goal, you need a PLAN — a systematic way of putting your goal into action. What are some of the first steps you can take?

Step 1: _____

_____

Step 2: _____

_____

Step 3: _____

_____

Step 4: _____

_____

One of the Nicest Things a Friend Ever Did for Me
A Circle Session

Objectives:
The students will:
—express the need to belong.
—describe how friends contribute to each other's enjoyment and well-being.

Introduce the Topic:
Today we're going to talk about the special moments that we have shared with our friends. Our topic is, "One of the Nicest Things a Friend Ever Did for Me."

Think of something that a friend did for you that you really appreciated. Perhaps it was totally spontaneous, like suddenly saying, "you're terrific." Or maybe it was carefully planned, like a surprise party or a special gift. Or your friend may simply have listened to you when you needed to talk. Some of the most meaningful moments between friends are simple and involve no money and almost no effort at all. Think about it for a few moments. The topic is, "One of the Nicest Things a Friend Ever Did for Me."

Discussion Questions:
1. What similarities or differences did you notice in the things we shared?
2. How can you show a friend that you appreciate what he or she has done for you?
3. How do you feel about asking a friend for help when you need it?

Something I Never Do When I Want to Make Friends
A Circle Session

Objectives:
The students will:
—express the need to belong.
—identify behaviors that can act as deterrents to friendship.

Introduce the Topic:
Making friends is kind of an art. There are things we can do that cause people to want to get to know us. And there are things we can do that are practically guaranteed to keep people away. Today, we're going to talk about the second group of behaviors — the roadblocks to friendship. Our topic is, "Something I Never Do When I Want to Make Friends."

What things do you purposely avoid doing if you like someone? Maybe you're careful not to be bossy or dominate conversations. Maybe you try not to be nosey, or make negative comments about what the person says or wears. Perhaps you've learned from experience that people are turned off by constant complaining or clowning around. Think about it for a few moments. The topic is, "Something I Never Do When I Want to Make Friends."

Discussion Questions:
1. Why do you avoid the behavior you mentioned?
2. Why is it important to know how to make friends?
3. What are the benefits and risks of telling others about the things they do that turn us off?
4. What can you do if you have trouble making friends and aren't sure why?

I Have a Friend Who Is Different From Me
A Circle Session

Objectives:
The students will:
—identify specific differences between themselves and their friends.
—demonstrate respect for differences in race, culture, lifestyle, and ability.

Introduce the Topic:
Today we are going to talk about friends who are different from us and what we like about them. The topic for this Sharing Circle is, "I Have a Friend Who Is Different From Me."

We are all alike in many ways, but we are also different. Today, I want you to think about a friend who is different from you in at least one major way — and tell us why you like this person so much. Perhaps your friend is of a different race, or has a much larger family, or is many years older than you. Does your friend speak a different language or eat a different way than you do? Does your friend have a disability that causes his or her lifestyle to be different from yours? Maybe your friend celebrates birthdays differently than you do, or has different holidays. Tell us what you enjoy about this person. Does your friend listen to you and share things with you? Does he or she invite you to go places? Do you have something in common, like a love of sports, music, or computers? Think about it for a few minutes. The topic is, "I Have a Friend Who Is Different From Me."

Discussion Questions:
1. What are some of the ways we differ from our friends?
2. How are you enriched by the differences between you and your friend?

Continued, next page

3. What causes people to dislike other people because of things like race or religion?
4. What would our lives be like if we could only make friends with people who are just like we are?

Help!
Experience Sheet and Discussion

Objectives:
The students will:
—differentiate between helpful and unhelpful "help."
—describe incidents in which they gave and received good and bad help.
—identify acceptable, empowering approaches to helping others.

Materials:
the experience sheet, "To Help of Not to Help;" chalkboard or chart paper

Directions:
Ask the students to picture in their minds the Laurel and Hardy classic in which Laurel tries to help Hardy with a ladder. In the process Laurel pokes out windows, hits Hardy on the head and knocks him down, breaks his wife's lamps and dishes, and finally totally destroys the entire house!

Point out to the students that this is an example of help — bad help! Good intentions, but bad help.

Involve the students in a discussion about help. Begin by saying something like this: *Help can be good to give and get. It can lift the weight off someone's back — or mind. Helping another person can be a generous thing to do. It can be brave and unselfish and is often instructive. Helping can cause the person who receives the help to feel grateful and the person who gives the help to feel rewarded. Helping can build friendships. However, sometimes help is given or received for the wrong reasons. Help is sometimes used as a way to gain power over another person. It can be used to insult someone or to interfere with his or her life. Unwelcome help can make a person feel resentful. Help that is forced on someone can make the person feel like a victim.*

Continued, next page

Ask the students to recall some of their own experiences. Ask them to recall a time when they had a task to complete or a problem to solve, and didn't feel like doing it alone. They *wanted* help, but they didn't really *need* help. They were perfectly capable of completing the job or solving the problem on your own. Invite volunteers to tell the group what happened and how they felt.

Next ask the students to think of a time when they may have *needed* help; for example, when they didn't know how to do something. But they didn't *want* the help, perhaps because they liked the challenge of having to figure it out alone, or were too proud to accept help. Again, invite volunteers to share their experiences.

Have the students turn to the experience sheet, "To Help or Not to Help." Give them approximately 10 to 15 minutes to complete the sheet, and then have the students form groups of four to six and share what they wrote. Allow about 15 minutes for sharing. Conclude the activity with a discussion involving the entire class.

Discussion Questions:
1. What did you learn about helping from this activity?
2. Do you tend to help others too much or not enough? Why do you think that is?
3. Is your answer the same when it comes to helping people with disabilities? If not, how and why is it different?
4. What is one specific thing you can do to become a better helper?

To Help or Not to Help
Experience Sheet

When you see someone who appears to need help, unless it is an obvious emergency, don't just jump in. First, find out if the person *wants* help. There's an important difference between needing help and wanting help.

How can you find out whether someone needs and/or wants help? One way is to ask. Another way is to quietly look at the situation and figure it out for yourself. Then if you feel that your help will be truly appreciated, offer it to the person. He or she can do one of two things — refuse the help or take it. It's that simple! But in offering help, be sure you're ready to accept either answer.

• Have you ever insisted on helping someone even though the person resisted your help? Describe what happened and how you and the other person felt about the situation and each other.

_____

_____

_____

_____

• Describe a time when you were forced to accept help that you didn't want. How did you feel about your "helper?" What did you do?

_____

_____

_____

_____

Good Help: Helping can be generous, instructive, courageous, and noble. It can improve friendships and bring people together. It can make a person more considerate of others and less self-centered. **Help is helpful when:**

1. It is needed and wanted.
2. It is given freely, and not rubbed in later.
3. Both the giver and receiver feel good about it.

• **Describe a time when you received good help.** _____

_____

_____

_____

Bad Help: Help can also be insulting and interfering. It can be used as a put down and a power tool. It can make a hero out of the giver, while the receiver feels resentful. **Help is unhelpful when:**

1. It causes more problems.
2. It is forced on a person who would rather solve his/her own problem.
3. When the giver is really after power or control.

• **Describe a time when you gave bad help.** _____

_____

_____

_____

Take a fun look at help. Recall a situation in your life, either amusing or serious, in which help was given, accepted, fouled up, or rejected. **Make a cartoon of it here:** ⟶

Someone Did Something for Me That I Appreciated
A Circle Session

Objectives:
The students will:
- describe a time when they received assistance and appreciated it.
— explain the dynamics of appreciation.
— differentiate between assistance that is wanted and unwanted.

Introduce the Topic:

Today's circle topic is, "Someone Did Something for Me That I Appreciated." Have you ever had someone do something for you that was out of the ordinary, unexpected, or particularly nice? Tell us about it.

The person could have been a member of your family, a teacher, or a friend. Maybe a brother or sister offered to help you with a difficult task, or a friend brought you a book to read when you were home with the flu. Perhaps you received an unexpected birthday greeting, or a phone call from someone who wanted to wish you good luck in a big game. Or maybe a teacher, family member, or friend taught you a skill that has enabled you to become more independent, such as how to do your own laundry, how to plan an event, or how to use a public transportation system. Think for a moment about something like this that's happened to you. If you let the person know how you felt, tell us about that, too. The topic for today is, "Someone Did Something for Me That I Appreciated."

Discussion Questions:
1. What similarities did you notice in the things we shared?
2. What enabled us to experience the emotion of appreciation?
3. Sometimes people do things for others that are *not* appreciated. How can that happen?

Continued, next page

3. If someone tries to do something for you against your wishes, what can you do about it?
4. If you want to do something for someone, how can you find out in advance whether or not your deed will be appreciated?

Something I Need Help With
A Circle Session

Objectives:
The students will:
—identify specific areas in which they need help.
—state that everyone needs help at one time or another.
—differentiate between constructive and destructive help.

Introduce the Topic:
Our Sharing Circle topic for today is, "Something I Need Help With." It simply is not possible to be self-sufficient at everything. There are times when all of us need some help. Describe one of those times for you.

Maybe you need help with a school subject, like math or foreign language. Or you might need help programming your VCR. Perhaps you could use some help understanding members of the opposite sex. Or maybe you want to become a good dancer, but feel totally clumsy. Do you need help overcoming a learning disability? Do you have a physical condition that requires regular medical attention? Maybe you need help to begin a good habit or quit a bad one. Everyone needs help with big things, and small things alike. Think about it for a moment, and tell us, "Something I Need Help With."

Discussion Questions:
1. What kinds of things do most of us seem to need help with?
2. What can you do to get the help you need?
3. Why do some people seem ashamed to ask for help?
4. Why do some people seem to look down on others who need help?
5. When is "help" not helpful?
6. What is the difference between constructive and destructive help?

I Helped Someone Who Needed and Wanted My Help
A Circle Session

Objectives:
The students will:
—describe incidents in which they played a helping role.
—name some of the characteristics of a helper.

Introduce the Topic:

Our topic today is, "I Helped Someone Who Needed and Wanted My Help." Can you think of a time when someone you knew obviously needed help? Perhaps the person was doing something incorrectly and you could see that; however, pride or stubbornness or self-determination wouldn't let him/her accept any help. You've also probably experienced times when people really wanted help, but didn't appear to need it. Perhaps they were just a little lazy and wanted your assistance to make things easier.

But can you recall of a time when someone both needed and wanted your help, and you were able to give it? Think about it for a few moments, and tell us about a time this happened in your life. Our topic is, "I Helped Someone Who Needed and Wanted My Help."

Discussion Questions:
1. How do most people feel when they get help that is both needed and wanted?
2. What does it take to be a good helper?
3. What feelings did you have when you realized that you could really help someone?

The Clique Phenomenon
Brainstorming, Discussion, and Experience Sheet

Objectives:
The students will:
—identify ways to make new friends.
—define the term *clique* and describe the effects of cliques.
—state how they can avoid making other people feel left out.

Materials:
the experience sheet, "Getting On Your Own Side;" chalkboard or chart paper

Directions:
Have the students form two teams. Give the teams 10 to 15 minutes to brainstorm a list describing as many ways as they can think of to make new friends. At the end of the allotted time, reconvene the class and ask the groups to share their lists. Possible ideas include:
- Sit beside someone different in the cafeteria and say hello.
- Offer to show someone new around the school.
- Join a school organization.
- Offer to help someone carry a heavy load.
- Team up with someone you don't know very well to work on a class project.
- Run an ad in the school paper asking for a companion for particular activities, like hiking or bicycling.
- Ask someone you know to introduce you to new people.
- Go to the gym or track after school and say hello to the kids who are practicing.

Write the word *clique* on the board and ask the students to help you define it. One possible definition might be:

An in-group or gang of kids that defines itself as much by who is excluded as by who is included.

Continued, next page

Discuss how a clique's policy of exclusion causes members to have difficulty making new friends, and can completely frustrate the efforts of someone who is not in the clique to become good friends with someone who is. Stress that the reason many kids want to be a part of a clique is that they want to be liked by "important" people and feel important themselves.

Ask the students to turn to the experience sheet, "Getting On Your Own Side." Allow the students about 10 minutes to complete the sheet. Then ask them to rejoin their teams and (voluntarily) share their answers to the questions.

Encourage the students to commit to making one new friend before the next session or to including one new person in their existing group of friends. Stipulate that before they can claim to have completed this assignment, the students must do something tangible with the new friend, such as sit together at an assembly, eat lunch together, go jogging or bicycling together, visit each other's home, see a movie together, or play video games after school. Ask the students to pay particular attention to the "clique phenomenon" and avoid doing anything that causes another person to feel left out. Conclude the activity with a discussion.

Discussion Questions:
1. In what ways do you think cliques are good?
2. In what ways do you think cliques are harmful?
3. Have you ever wanted to belong to a clique? If so, why was it important?
4. What would happen if there were no cliques at this school?
5. What kinds of cliques do adults have?

Getting on Your Own Side
Experience Sheet

Is it worth it to be in?

What have you done to be included in a group?

I have...

___Yes ___No • risked losing friends.

___Yes ___No • hurt people who thought they were my friends by making them feel left out.

___Yes ___No • done something I thought was not right.

___Yes ___No • done something I knew was against the law.

___Yes ___No • drunk alcohol or used drugs.

___Yes ___No • done something that might have harmed me physically.

___Yes ___No • done something that cost me a lot of money.

___Yes ___No • done something that interfered with my school work.

___Yes ___No • done something my parents would have objected to if they had known.

___Yes ___No • done whatever was necessary, as long as it didn't harm anyone else.

___Yes ___No • done something that was against my religion.

___Yes ___No • done whatever was necessary.

Can you remember a time when you were pressured to exclude someone from an activity?

How did you feel? _____

_____

_____

_____

_____

What did you do? _____

_____

_____

_____

_____

If this ever happens again, what do you think you will do? _____

_____

_____

_____

_____

_____

How It Feels To Be Left Out
Creative Writing and Discussion

Objectives:

The students will:

—describe in writing how a person might feel in response to being excluded.

—describe behavioral choices available in response to rejection/ exclusion.

Materials:

writing materials

Directions:

Explain to the students that you would like them to write about the topic, "How It Feels to Be Left Out." Emphasize that they will need to use their imaginations, because they are going to write from the viewpoint of a person of a different race or culture, or a person with a disability.

In your own words, explain to the students: *Imagine a situation in which a person might be excluded. Think about how you feel when you are left out of a group or activity that you really want to participate in. How might the situation and/or the feelings be the same or different for someone of a different race or culture, or someone with a disability? If the feelings would be about the same, what would they be? If the feelings would be different, how would they be different, and what would they be like? You might begin your story when the person is just starting to think about joining the group or activity. Describe what happens that leads to the rejection, and concentrate on the expression of feelings throughout.*

Ask the students to indicate at the end of their papers whether or not they would be willing to read their story to the class. Collect the papers and evaluate them in your usual manner, then return them to the students. Suggest that the students rewrite their papers as homework. At a subsequent class meeting, ask volunteers to read their stories to the class. Facilitate a discussion after each reading, basing your questions on issues presented in the story. Conclude the activity with a general discussion.

Discussion Questions:
1. How are the feelings of most people the same in response to rejection? How are they different for people who belong to a minority race or culture? ...for people who have a disability?
2. What did you discover about your own attitudes towards people who belong to minorities or have disabilities?
3. What good does it do to try to understand each other's feelings?
4. What new ideas did you get about rejecting others? ...about handling rejection? ...about the idea of inclusion?

Pigeonholes and Stereotypes
Experiments with Labeling Language

Objectives:
The students will:
—identify specific labels used to stereotype individuals and
   groups.
—invent stereotyping labels for themselves and others in the
   group.
—describe the negative effects of stereotyping labels.

Materials:
chalkboard or chart paper

Directions:
   Talk to the students about the dehumanization caused by
spoken and written language habits that either fail to promote
individuality or associate people with stereotyping labels. Ask
the students to help you brainstorm a list of stereotyping language. Write all ideas on the board. Include the following
examples:

Groups of people are stereotyped by labels such as:
   • The old   • The handicapped
   • Those foreigners   • The homeless
   • The retarded`   • The blacks

Individuals are stereotyped by labels such as:
   • A TMR (Trainable Mentally Retarded)
   • An Illegal alien
   • A welfare mother
   • A Quad (Quadriplegic)

Many times, individuals or groups are referred to using archaic
terms:
   • Coloreds   • Illegitimate children
   • Morons   • Mongoloids
   • Spastics

Continued, next page

Point out that the simplest solution to this problem is to remember that every individual is a *person* first, and to make a conscious effort to refer to people as people. Suggest that if labels cannot be avoided, they should be used as descriptive parts of speech, not as subjects (nouns). For example:
- "Roger is African American."
- "Grace is a person who is homeless."
- "Cindy is a person with Cerebral Palsy."
- "Ruben has a learning disability."
- "Lucy receives welfare."

Ask the students to consider the fact that they label others every day. Give a graphic example by moving past the group in a way that would be considered pretty ordinary except for the repetition of some small quirk, tick, or unusual move. Then ask the group: *How might you or other students label me? How would you refer to me in your conversations?*

Have the students form small groups of four to six. Ask them to take a couple of minutes to think about how others see them and to come up with a short label (one to three words) for themselves based on *how they think others see them.* Have the students take turns introducing themselves to the group using their first name and the label. (Examples: "Hi, I'm Aloof and Distant Denise" or "My name is Alex the Android.")

Next, direct the students to turn to the person on their right and observe that person silently for a moment or two. Have them think of a one-word label for the person based on their observations. Ask the students to combine the label with the person's first name and share it with the group. Examples might be, "Fat Frank" or "Queen Donna."

Finally, have the students pair up within their groups. Direct the partners to interview each other for 4 minutes (2 minutes each) before coming up with a one to three-word label for their partner based on what they learned in the interview. Direct the students to introduce their partner to the group using the partner's first name plus the label.

In a follow-up discussion, ask the students to share with the entire group their feelings about the labels they gave and received.

Discussion Questions:

1. How did you feel when you labeled yourself?
2. How did you feel when you were labeled by someone else?
3. How did you feel when *you* labeled someone else?
4. How often do we label others and why do we do it?
5. What effect does labeling have on our self-esteem? ...on our ability to really know one another? ...on our efforts to include all kinds of people?
6. What can we do to become more aware of our tendency to label others? How can we reverse that tendency?

Promoting Inclusion
A Brainstorming Activity

Objectives:
The students will:
—learn and practice a brainstorming process.
—name specific ways individuals can demonstrate the value of inclusion.
—describe significant contributions to inclusion and state who made them.

Materials:
chalkboard and chalk; stopwatch or watch with secondhand

Directions:
Begin with a discussion about the concept of *inclusion*. Point out that a state of full inclusion is the opposite of a situation in which individuals or groups of people are excluded from full participation in society — whether the exclusion takes place in housing, work, education, health care, leisure, government, or any other area. Ask the students if they value inclusion. Most will say yes. Then write this assignment on the board:

- Name all the ways you can think of for us to communicate to others our value of inclusion.
- Name as many people as you can think of who have contributed to inclusion in some way and describe how they did it. They can be people you know, public figures, or historical figures.

Announce that the class as a whole is going to brainstorm these two lists. Get agreement on the following rules for brainstorming:

1. Think of as many possible suggestions as you can in the allotted time.
2. Use your imagination and be creative.
3. Do not question, criticize, or evaluate any suggestion during the brainstorming process.

4. After the brainstorming period is closed, go back and evaluate/discuss the suggestions.
5. Agree on a final list.

Announce that the students will have 3 minutes to brainstorm each list. Appoint a timekeeper and begin brainstorming the first list. Record suggested items on the board. At the end of 3 minutes, brainstorm the second list. When time is up, go back and discuss the items on the first list, achieving consensus on a final list. Do the same with the second list. Suggest that the students judge the items on the first list based on whether or not they are doable, and on whether or not they will achieve the goal (communicating the value of inclusion). Evaluate each name on the second list based on the suggested person's deeds and the impact of those deeds.

Display the final lists on a bulletin board. Complete the activity with a class discussion.

Discussion Questions:
1. Why is it important to know how to communicate the things we value to others?
2. If we don't communicate the values we have, how will others

Strength in Numbers
Small Group Experiment and Discussion

Objectives:
The students will:
—demonstrate the principle of collective strength.
—demonstrate that interdependence doesn't mean giving up individual identity.
—identify the benefits of having a support group.
—reinforce identification with a group.

Materials:
3/16" wooden dowels, twelve inches in length (two per student); assorted ribbon, string, or twine; small paper tags with strings attached

Directions:
Form groups of six to twelve students, or use existing work groups. Have each group select a leader to be in charge of the materials for the activity. Instruct the group leaders to give each member of their group one dowel.

Explain to the students that their dowels represent themselves, and should be thought of as having all the strengths, vulnerabilities, and feelings that they as individuals have. Explain that the pressures and stresses experienced by people as they journey through life can cause individuals to bend — and sometimes even break. Instruct the students to start bending their dowels to see how much pressure the dowels can take before breaking. (Have each group assist any of its members who have difficulty due to insufficient strength or dexterity.)

After all of the students have broken their dowels, ask for a show of hands from individuals indicating how much pressure was required — very little, moderate, or extreme. Point out that some people were able to break their dowels easily while more effort was required by others. Explain that individuals are able to withstand life pressures to different degrees as well. How much stress an individual can withstand depends on how effectively he or she is able to cope with stress. However, even the strongest person can break.

Ask the leaders to give their group members the remaining dowels (one each) along one small tag per member. Ask the students to write their name on their tag. Have the students attach the tag to their dowel. Then ask the leaders to collect their group's dowels and tie them into a bundle with the ribbon or twine. Now ask the leaders to try to break the bundle of dowels using only their hands. (Demonstrate by briefly borrowing a bundle from one of the groups and attempting to break it.) Allow each group member to take a turn trying to break the bundle. Point out that even a very strong person would have extreme difficulty with the task. Lead a follow-up discussion.

Discussion questions:
1. What is the difference between individual identity and group identity?
2. What are some advantages of working in groups?
3. How does having a support group make it easier to withstand the pressures of life? ...to accomplish a task?
4. What does it mean to be interdependent?
5. What happens to individual identity when a person becomes a member of a group?
5. What are some areas in which support groups can have value?

Variation:
If a group has been working together long enough to have established a collective name and identity, ask that group to label its bundle with a 5 x 7 note card decorated with its logo or name. If a group is newly formed, this might be a good time to create a group name/identity.

Linked Together
Creating a Symbolic Chain

Objectives:
The students will:
—graphically symbolize a unique gift/talent they possess.
—verbally and nonverbally acknowledge the gifts/talents of class members.
—demonstrate understanding that strength exists in diversity.

Materials:
light-weight bristol board or poster paper (sturdy, but flexible) cut into 2-inch by 10-inch strips (one per student, plus a few extras); marking pens in various colors; stapler and staples

Directions:
Begin this activity by asking the students to recall and reiterate some of the ways in which groups rely on the talents and skills of all members. Ask the students to explain how utilizing everyone's gifts and talents can make the class a better place to learn.

In your own words, explain that the strength and unity within a class can be compared to a chain with many individual links. If each link represents a different strength, uniting the links creates a chain that is longer and much stronger than any single link could ever be alone. Similarly, uniting gifts and talents in the class makes the group stronger by allowing every individual to benefit from the strength of every other individual. Ask the students to comment and to share their own ideas and insights.

Distribute the paper strips and colored marking pens. Explain that each strip represents a "link" in the class chain. Ask the students to use the markers to letter their name on the strip, and to add a graphic symbol that represents a talent or skill they contribute to the class. The symbol can be as literal or abstract as they wish, just as long as they can verbalize what it represents. Allow approximately 15 minutes for lettering and art work. Encourage collaboration. Create a link for yourself.

Have the students join you to form one large circle. Go around the circle and ask each member to hold up his/her link and explain the meaning of his/her graphic symbol. After the first and second persons share, give them the stapler and ask them to form their links into interlocking circles. After the third person shares, have that person attach his/her link to the "chain." Pass the stapler to each new person who shares so that the chain grows longer and longer and is finally linked together by the last person who shares. Hang the chain somewhere in the room. In a follow-up discussion, ask the students to talk about the symbolism of the activity.

Discussion Questions:
1. What does our chain represent to you?
2. How do you feel knowing that you are symbolically linked to every member of the class?
3. How can we translate our symbolic links into actual behavior on a day-to-day basis?
4. What have you learned from this activity?

Go Team!
Game Series and Discussion

Objectives:
the students will:
—demonstrate teamwork by playing three cooperative games.
—use teamwork to solve problems encountered during the games.
—identify specific behaviors that contribute to and detract from teamwork.

Materials:
optional camera with film

Directions:
A couple of these games can be used quite literally to "build" a team. All three require cooperative efforts and develop synergism. Play the games on a grassy area outdoors or in a large room with tumbling mats. Announce a "game day," and play the games as a series, or intersperse them among the other activities in this unit. Involve everyone. Require that the teams themselves solve any problems that arise during the games. Discussion questions are provided for use after a single game or all three.

Game 1: "Stand Up Together"

Players:
minimum of 2

Directions:
Players divide into pairs. Partners sit on the ground, back-to-back, knees bent and elbows linked. From that position, partners lean in unison against each other's back and slowly push with the legs to get to a standing position. Struggling, stumbling, and giggling is expected until partners get the feel of how to balance themselves and move as a unit. Once the move is mastered in pairs, add a third person to each group, then

another, and another. The game can also be played with a large group standing shoulder-to-shoulder tightly in a circle. However, unless the whole group is seriously concentrating on the task, be ready to witness more giggling and stumbling than standing!

Game 2: "People Pyramids"

Players:
6 or more

Directions:
Form teams of six and proceed as follows: The three huski-est players line up shoulder-to-shoulder on their hands and knees, keeping their backs straight. The two next-huskiest players carefully climb onto the backs of the first three. Each of these players straddles two of the lower players, placing hands on the shoulders and knees and feet on the backs (next to, but not on the spine) of the lower players. The lightest person tops off the pyramid by climbing on and straddling the two middle players. Players try to "hold" the position for at least 15 sec-onds, allowing enough time to snap a picture of the pyramid if a camera is available. To break up the pyramid, players collapse and roll toward the outside of the configuration. A group of 10 can make a larger pyramid, with four on the bottom, then three, two, and one. Ambitious groups can make a castle by creating a circular base with players facing inward and two to three layers on top.

Game 3: "Untying the Knot"

Players:
12 and up

Directions:
Players stand in a circle, shoulder-to-shoulder, and place their hands in the center. Every player grasps two hands. Players must *not* hold both hands of the same person, or hold the hand of a person right next to them. (Doing either of these

things will create a permanent tangle.) Everyone is responsible for making sure that the "knot" is "tied" correctly.

There are two basic approaches to "untying the knot." One is through the trial and error process of going under, over, and through other players in hopes of hitting upon the solution. The other is to carefully survey the situation and then instruct each player precisely where to move and in what order. Allow the players to come to some agreement as to which approach to use. When at last the knot is unraveled, players will find themselves in one large circle (occasionally, two interconnected circles). During the untangling process, the team may come upon one or two connections that defy solution. When this happens, they must decide whether or not to break hands momentarily so that the game can proceed.

Discussion Questions:
1. Which game did you like best and why?
2. How well did you work together *as a team* during the games?
3. What kinds of problems did you encounter as a team and how did you resolve them?
4. What did you learn about teamwork from this activity?

I Wanted to Be Part of a Group, But Was Left Out
A Circle Session

Objectives:
The students will:
—understand and express the need to belong.
—describe an incident in which they were excluded.
—explain how the need to belong can influence individual behavior.

Introduce the Topic:

One of the most important things to most young people is fitting in — belonging to a group. Although this need continues into adulthood, it is particularly strong among young people, because this is the time when the skills of group membership are learned. It is one of the main "developmental tasks" of youth. Today, we're going to look at what happens when we are refused membership in a group for some reason. We're going to talk about the feelings we experience when we are excluded. Our topic is, "I Wanted to Be Part of a Group, But Was Left Out."

Think back to a time when you really wanted to do something with a group of friends or an organization, but you weren't invited. How did you feel? What did you do? Maybe you tried out for a part in a play or a musical group and didn't make it. How long did it take you to get over it? Have you ever heard some friends talking about something fun they did over the weekend and felt hurt because you weren't asked to join them? Have you ever tried to join in a conversation and been completely ignored? Have you ever felt that you were excluded because you were poorer than the other members of the group, or of a different race, or had a disability? Think about it for a few moments. If you decide to share, describe the situation and tell us how you handled your feelings. Our topic is, "I Wanted to Be Part of a Group, But Was Left Out."

Discussion Questions:
1. What did you feel like doing when you were left out? What *did* you do?
2. How long did it take you to get over your hurt feelings?
3. If a group rejects you because you refuse to conform to its code of behavior, what's the best thing to do?
4. What advice would you give a friend who seemed willing to do almost anything to fit in with a group?
5. How do attitudes of exclusion hurt us?
6. What can you do to develop an attitude of inclusion?

Conflict du Jour
Observations and Discussion

Objectives:
The students will:
—describe five conflicts that they have observed.
—identify and evaluate the conflict-resolution strategies and
  methods used.

Materials:
one copy of the "Conflict Observation Form" for each student;
chalkboard and chalk

Directions:
Distribute copies of the "Conflict Observation Form."

Explain that the students are to observe five conflicts, one
each day for a week. The observed conflicts may occur between students at school, family members at home, characters
on a TV show, etc.

Stress that the students are not to get involved; they are to
observe silently. After each conflict, the students should immediately record their observations and answer the questions on
the form.

The following week, ask the students to take out their completed observation forms. Have them form groups of four to six
and share their observations. Ask the groups to tally the number of times each method or strategy was used to end a conflict.
Have the groups report their findings, while you record numbers
and observations on the board. Facilitate discussion.

Discussion Questions:
1. How did you feel when you were observing other people's
   conflicts?
2. What kinds of things did people most often do that were
   helpful?

Continued, next page

3. What kinds of things did people do that were harmful?
4. What kinds of things were least effective?
5. How will your own methods of handling conflict change as a result of completing this activity?

Extension:

Have the students role play some of the conflicts — first using the resolution/ending they observed, and then using a more effective strategy.

Conflict Observation Sheet

Directions: Observe one conflict every day for a week. As soon as you can after the conflict has ended, write down your answers to the following questions.

What was the conflict about?	How many people were involved?	Describe what happened:

MONDAY

Check all methods used to resolve or end the conflict: ____ fight or argument ____ putting it off ____ apologizing ____ sharing or taking turns

____ humor ____ compromise ____ asking for help ____ problem solving or negotiation ____ other:

TUESDAY

Check all methods used to resolve or end the conflict: ____ fight or argument ____ putting it off ____ apologizing ____ sharing or taking turns

____ humor ____ compromise ____ asking for help ____ problem solving or negotiation ____ other:

WEDNESDAY

Check all methods used to resolve or end the conflict: ____ fight or argument ____ putting it off ____ apologizing ____ sharing or taking turns

____ humor ____ compromise ____ asking for help ____ problem solving or negotiation ____ other:

What was the conflict about?	How many people were involved?	Describe what happened:

THURSDAY

Check all methods used to resolve or end the conflict: ____fight or argument ____putting it off ____apologizing ____sharing or taking turns

____humor ____compromise ____asking for help ____problem solving or negotiation ____other: _____

FRIDAY

Check all methods used to resolve or end the conflict: ____fight or argument ____putting it off ____apologizing ____sharing or taking turns

____humor ____compromise ____asking for help ____problem solving or negotiation ____other: _____

SATURDAY/SUNDAY

Check all methods used to resolve or end the conflict: ____fight or argument ____putting it off ____apologizing ____sharing or taking turns

____humor ____compromise ____asking for help ____problem solving or negotiation ____other: _____

Conflicts, Adult Style
Interviews and Discussion

Objectives:
The students will:
—interview people regarding conflicts they have had.
—identify and evaluate strategies used to resolve conflicts.

Materials:
at least one copy of the interview form, "Conflicts Happen" for each student

Directions:
Announce that the students are going to conduct interviews with adults about conflicts they have had. The person inter-viewed could be a parent, other relative, neighbor, friend, teacher, religious leader, or coach.

Distribute the interview forms. Explain that side one of the form is for use *during* the interview; side two is for the student to complete *after* the interview. Stress that the students are to listen with particular care to *how* the conflict was resolved. If they don't understand what their interviewee is saying, urge the students to ask questions for clarification. Demonstrate effec-tive ways of seeking additional information (open-ended ques-tions, summarizing, etc.). Set a deadline for completion of the interviews.

Have the students share their findings in groups of four to six. Tell them not to identify the people in the conflict. Suggest that they refer to them as persons A and B, or give them ficti-tious names. Conclude the activity with a class discussion.

Discussion Questions:
1. What kinds of things seem to lead to conflict?
2. What similarities did you hear in the ways people react to conflict?

Continued, next page

3. What methods were most often used to resolve these conflicts?
4. What methods seemed to be most effective?
5. In cases where the conflict was never resolved, how do the people feel now?
6. In cases where the conflict was resolved negatively (for instance, through a fight or one person getting back at the other), how do the people feel now?
7. What have you learned about conflict from this activity?

Conflicts Happen!
Interview Form

Ask an adult to tell you about a conflict he or she had with another person. Write down the adult's answers to these questions. Pay special attention to *how* the conflict was resolved:

1. How did the conflict start? _____

_____

2. What was the conflict about? _____

_____

_____

3. What was it that you needed or wanted? _____

_____

4. What did the other person need or want?_____

_____

5. Was the conflict resolved? _____ If so, how? _____

_____

_____

6. Were you satisfied with the outcome of the conflict?_____

Why or why not? _____

_____

_____

Which of the following methods were used to resolve the conflict. Put a ✔ beside <u>all</u> that apply.

_____ Nothing was done, so the conflict was never resolved.

_____ One or both people apologized.

_____ Both people gave up a little of what they wanted, arriving at a *compromise*.

_____ Both people thought of possible solutions, talked them over, and agreed to try the one that sounded best. (*Negotiation* and *Problem Solving*)

_____ One person listened while the other person expressed his or her feelings. Just listening made things better.

_____ One person said something funny and the other person laughed. The humor made both people feel better and the conflict wasn't so important anymore.

_____ One person offered to share or take turns, and the other person accepted.

_____ Other _____

_____

_____

_____

_____

_____

_____

Conflicts I've Managed
Dyads and Discussion

Objectives:
The students will:
—describe conflict resolution strategies they have used.
—discuss the effectiveness of conflict resolution strategies in different situations.

Materials:
chart paper and magic markers or chalkboard and chalk

Directions:
Ask the students to choose partners and sit facing each other. Tell the partners to get as far away from other pairs as possible, to reduce distractions. Explain that you are going to give them several topics that involve the use of conflict management strategies. Both partners will speak for 2 minutes on each topic. Tell the students that you will call time every 2 minutes. Urge them not to interrupt each other or ask unnecessary questions. Suggest they alternate being the first speaker.

Announce the topics one at a time, writing them on chart paper or the chalkboard. Briefly discuss the intent of each topic and give examples, as needed. (See suggestions in parentheses, below.)

Topics
"I Shared Something I Wanted for Myself"
   (Children are admonished to share starting at a very young age. At what point do they recognize that sharing prevents/resolves conflict, and choose to share of their own accord.)

"A Time Somebody Was Mad at Me, But Calmed Down After I Listened to Him/Her"
   (This topic relates to the effectiveness of active listening in diffusing strong feelings, whereas arguing, criticizing, and blaming generally aggravate them.)

Continued, next page

"A Time I Apologized, But I Didn't Take the Blame"
(This topic is intended to illustrate that a person can express regret and sympathy, while making it clear that s/he did not cause the problem.)

"It Looked As If a Fight Might Start, So We Put It Off"
(This topic is based on the notion that when one or both persons in a conflict are tired or overcome by negative feelings, a wise strategy is often to postpone any discussion until a later time.)

"Instead of Fighting, We Ended Up Laughing"
(This topic addresses the effectiveness of humor, jokes, and clowning in conflict situations.)

"A Time I Managed a Conflict by Negotiating or Compromising"
(This topic suggests that both parties may be able to win in a conflict situation if they are willing to participate in problem solving, or are willing to *give up* part of what they want in order to *get* part of what they want.)

Reconvene the class. Facilitate a class discussion.

Discussion Questions:
1. Which conflict resolution strategy have you used most often? ...least often? Why?
2. What happens when you try to ignore a conflict?
3. What can you do if the other person refuses to try to resolve the conflict?
4. Which of these strategies can be used by a third party who is acting as a mediator in a conflict situation?

Exploring Alternatives to Conflict
Dramatizations and Discussion

Objectives:
The students will:
—learn and practice specific strategies for resolving conflict.

Materials:
a copy of one scenario (from the list below) for each group of students; one copy of the experience sheet, "Conflict Resolution Strategies," for each student

Directions:
Distribute the experience sheet, "Conflict Resolution Strategies." On the board, write the heading "Strategies for Resolving Conflict." Explain to the students that in conflict situations, certain kinds of behaviors tend to help people solve their problems. List the strategies shown below, while the students follow along on their experience sheets. Give examples, and ask the students to describe problems that might be resolved by each alternative.

- **Sharing:** Using/doing something with another person.
- **Taking turns:** Alternately using/doing something with another person.
- **Active Listening:** Hearing the other person's feelings or opinions.
- **Postponing:** Deciding to put off dealing with the conflict until another time.
- **Using humor:** Looking at the situation in a comical way; making light of the situation.
- **Compromising:** Giving up part, in order to get the remainder, of what one wants.
- **Expressing regret:** Saying that you are sorry about the situation, without taking the blame.
- **Problem solving:** Discussing the problem; trying to find a mutually acceptable solution.

Continued, next page

Divide the class into small groups and give each group a written conflict scenario. Instruct the groups to discuss the scenario and pick a conflict management strategy from the list of alternatives on the board. Have the members of each group act out the conflict and its resolution, while the rest of the class tries to guess which alternative they are using. At the conclusion of the role plays, lead a class discussion.

Discussion Questions:

1. Why is it better to practice positive alternatives, rather than wait for a conflict to occur and *then* try them?
2. Which strategies are hardest to use and why? Which are easiest? Which work best and why?
3. When do you think you should get help to resolve a conflict?

Conflict Scenarios

Your group is working on a geography project. You are using the computer to develop a series of charts showing facts about different countries. As a final step, you plan to use a graphics program to draw illustrations for the charts. However, another group member also wants to do the illustrations. The two of you start arguing about who should get the job and other group members take sides. The situation becomes very tense and noisy and the project is in danger of being ruined. Your teacher approaches the group and warns you to solve the problem — or forget the project.

You plan to go to the movies on Saturday afternoon with a friend. Your family suddenly decides to hold a yard clean-up on Saturday, and this makes you very upset. You start to argue with your parents, insisting that since you have done your homework and chores all week, you deserve to spend Saturday afternoon at the movie. Besides, your friend's parents have agreed to let the two of use their car. You are in danger of being put on restriction because you are starting to yell at your parents.

Without realizing it, you dropped (and lost) your homework on the way to school. That has put you in a bad mood. In gym, a classmate accidently hits you in the back with a soccer ball.

You react in anger and threaten to beat up your classmate after school. This makes the classmate angry and he or she reluctantly agrees to fight. Other classmates take sides and are talking about staying after school to watch the fight. During lunch, you have a chance to think about it. Your realize that you picked the fight because you were upset about your lost homework. You didn't like being hit by the ball, but think that maybe it isn't worth a fight.

You make plans with a few friends to meet a half hour before school to play a quick game of basketball. You get up early, but decide to watch TV instead of meeting your friends. When you get to school, your friends are angry. They say you messed up the game by making one of the teams a person short. They want you to know that you let them down. Before they can express their feelings, you start making excuses. You don't give them a chance to talk. They start to walk away.

Two students share a locker at school. One of the students is in a rush one day and unknowingly leaves the locker open. When the second student discovers the open locker an hour later, a jacket, a pair of sneakers, and a cassette tape are missing. The second student blames the first, who denies responsibility. They start to fight.

Conflict Resolution Strategies
Experience Sheet

Have you ever been in a conflict? Of course! No matter how much you try to avoid them, conflicts happen. They are part of life. What makes conflicts upsetting is not knowing how to handle them. If you don't know something helpful to do, you may end up making things worse. So study these strategies, and the next time you see a conflict coming, try one!

1. Share.
Whatever the conflict is over, keep (or use) some of it yourself, and let the other person have or use some.

2. Take turns.
Use or do something for a little while. Then let the other person take a turn.

3. Active Listen.
Let the other person talk while you listen carefully. Really try to understand the person's feelings and ideas.

4. Postpone.
If you or the other person are very angry or tired, put off dealing with the conflict until another time.

5. Use humor.
Look at the situation in a comical way. Don't take it too seriously.

6. Compromise.
Offer to give up part of what you want and ask the other person to do the same.

7. Express regret.
Say that you are sorry about the situation, *without* taking the blame.

8. Problem solve.
Discuss the problem and try to find a solution that is acceptable to both you and the other person.

I Observed a Conflict
A Circle Session

Objectives:
The students will:
—describe a conflict situation they observed.
—discuss the dynamics of conflict.
—describe feelings generated in conflict situations.

Introduce the Topic:
Today we're going to talk about conflict situations we've witnessed. Our topic is, "I Observed a Conflict."

There probably isn't anyone here who hasn't at some point in his or her life watched some kind of conflict taking place. A conflict can take many forms. It can be an argument between two people over who has the best idea for a project, or who gets to choose which T.V. show to watch. It can be a squabble over who gets the last cookie. Some conflicts are fights or arguments that involve some kind of violence or the threat of it. Still other conflicts take place inside one person; for example, when someone is torn between two choices, like who to vote for, what to do on the weekend, or who to live with after a divorce. Think of a conflict that you observed. It could have been between friends, family members, or strangers. Without actually telling us who was involved, or your relationship to the people, tell us what happened. The topic is, "I Observed a Conflict."

Discussion Questions:
1. Why do we have conflicts?
2. What kinds of things happened in most of the conflicts we shared?
3. Why is it sometimes difficult to think clearly when you get involved in an argument?
4. Is it possible for both people to win in a conflict? How?

I Got Into a Conflict
A Circle Session

Objectives:
The students will:
—describe conflicts they have experienced and what caused them.
—describe ways of dealing with the feelings of others in conflict situations.
—identify strategies for resolving conflicts with peers and adults.

Introduce the Topic:
Our topic today is, "I Got Into a Conflict." Conflicts are very common. They occur because of big and little things that happen in our lives. And sometimes the littlest things that happen can lead to the biggest conflicts. This is your opportunity to talk about a time when you had an argument or fight with someone. Maybe you and a friend argued over something that one of you said that the other didn't like. Or maybe you argued with a brother or sister over what TV show to watch, or who should do a particular chore around the house. Have you ever had a fight because someone broke a promise or couldn't keep as secret? If you feel comfortable telling us what happened, we'd like to hear it. Describe what the other person did and said, and what you did and said. Tell us how you felt and how the other person seemed to feel. There's just one thing you shouldn't tell us and that's the name of the other person, okay? Take a few moments to think about it. The topic is, "I Got Into a Conflict."

Discussion Questions:
1. How did most of us feel when we were part of a conflict?
2. What kinds of things led to the conflicts that we shared?
3. How could some of our conflicts have been prevented?
4. What conflict management strategies could have been used in the situations that we shared?

When One Person Kept Blaming Another for Causing a Problem
A Circle Session

Objectives:
The students will:
—describe a time when blaming perpetuated a conflict.
—state why blaming is counterproductive to conflict resolution.

Introduce the Topic:
Today in our circle, we're going to talk about times when we were part of the "blame game." Our topic is, "When One Person Kept Blaming Another for Causing a Problem."

Blaming is something we are all tempted to do at times. But it usually isn't very helpful. Saying a problem is someone else's fault may get us out of trouble, but it usually doesn't solve the problem. Can you think of a time when you saw one person blame another for just about every part of a problem? Maybe you know someone who gets in trouble a lot and always says it's someone else's fault. Or maybe you have a brother or sister who blames you for just about every problem that comes up at home. Have you heard government leaders who always seem to be blaming each other instead of taking responsibility? Have you tried to settle fights between younger children in which it was hard to figure out what happened because each child blamed the other? Think about it for a few moments. Tell us what happened and how you felt, but don't use any names. The topic is, "When One Person Kept Blaming Another for Causing a Problem."

Discussion Questions:
1. Why is blaming not a helpful thing to do?
2. How do you feel when someone blames you for something?
3. If you're trying to help two people settle a conflict, how can you get them to stop blaming each other?

A Time We Needed Help to Resolve a Conflict
A Circle Session

Objectives:

The students will:

—describe a conflict in which the help of a third party was needed.

—identify helpful behaviors on the part of a conflict mediator.

Introduce the Topic:

Our topic for this session is, "A Time We Needed Help to Resolve a Conflict." All of us get into conflicts with our family and friends. Much of the time, we work things out without getting anyone else involved. But sometimes a conflict is too big or too upsetting to handle without help. Can you remember such a time? Maybe you and a brother or sister were arguing over whose turn it was to mow the lawn, and you had to ask one of your parents to help figure it out. Or maybe you had a conflict with a friend over something you were told he or she said about you behind your back, and it took the help of another friend to get the two of you back together. Perhaps you and a classmate had to ask the teacher to settle an argument over who had the correct answer to a problem, or maybe you had to let your coach help settle a fight between you and a teammate. Think about it for a few moments, and tell us what the conflict was about and what the third person did to help you settle it. The topic is, "A Time We Needed Help to Resolve a Conflict."

Discussion Questions:

1. What were some of the reasons we had to ask for help?
2. When is it a good idea to let someone else help you resolve a conflict?
3. If you ask for help resolving a conflict and the person you ask just comes over and tells you what to do, is that helpful? Why or why not?
4. What kind of help *is* helpful in resolving a conflict?

Search for the One Person Team
Group Discussion and Experience Sheet

Objectives:
The students will:
—state that successful teams are characterized by diversity.
—identify specific differences that have contributed to a
   successful group endeavor.
—distinguish between individual and group identity.
—distinguish between interdependence and dependence.

Materials:
one copy of the experience sheet "Search for the One-Person
Team" for each student

Directions:
Introduce the experience sheet by making the point that
rarely is a successful endeavor accomplished by one person
acting alone. Even when a single individual appears to have
masterminded and carried out a project single-handedly, there
are always other people in the background without whose cooperation and collaboration the finished product would not have
been achieved.

Announce to the students that you want each of them to
identify a group that is diverse and interdependent, and identify
the different skills and talents that make the group successful.
Explain that the students may choose any type of group they
wish: a band, singing group, athletic team, club, business, etc.
The group may be one to which they belong, or it may be a
group they have observed in action or read about. A solo per-
former who works with a backup team or a support crew may
also be considered a group.

Have the students turn to the experience sheet, "Search for
the One-Person Team," and announce that they will have about
15 minutes to complete the sheet.

Continued, next page

When the students have completed their experience sheets, ask volunteers to tell the class about the diverse make-up of the group they selected. After those students who wish to have shared, make the following points:

- No one can succeed in complete isolation.
- We all have gifts to contribute and those gifts are needed somewhere.
- Generally speaking, teams accomplish more than individuals accomplish.
- When we choose to be *interdependent* with others, we are not becoming a *dependent* person, we are joining our resources with the resources of others in a common effort.

Conclude the activity by facilitating further discussion.

Discussion Questions:

1. What is the difference between interdependence and dependence?
2. How does diversity make a group successful?
3. When you think about the group or team you selected, do you judge the group by thinking about individual members or by thinking about the group as a whole? Why do you think that is?
4. Can you think of a person who succeeded at something without "interdepending" with others?

Search for the One-Person Team
Experience Sheet

When people come together, they bring all of their unique personalities, viewpoints, talents, and skills. When they use these differences to work toward a common goal, wonderful things often happen. Take a moment to think of some groups and teams that you know about. Pick a group or team that you think is successful because each member brings something special and important to the process. Then answer the following questions:

What is the name of the group?_____

What does the group do? _____

What talents or skills do members of the group have?_____

_____

_____

Can you name all the members of this group? Name and describe as many as you can:

Name	Description
1. _____	_____
2. _____	_____
3. _____	_____
4. _____	_____
5. _____	_____

What makes this group stand out?_____

_____

What's Your Preference — Alone or Together?

Team Experiment and Discussion

Objectives:

The students will:

—demonstrate the power of team efforts.

—describe advantages of working with a team. ...of working alone.

—identify their preferred way of working — alone or with a group.

Materials:

a stop watch or watch/clock with a second hand; chalkboard and chalk; writing materials for each student

Directions:

Have the students form teams of four or five. From the following list, select one word for each team. Write the assigned words on the board so all of the groups can see their word.

identification
reverberation
heterogeneous
responsiveness
haberdasher
refrigeration
significantly
predetermination
simultaneous

Explain to the students that, *working individually,* they are to write as many words as they can, using the letters in the word that has been assigned to them. Go over the rules, saying: *There will be NO talking. You must write real words of two or more letters using only the letters in the assigned word. For example, if your assigned word contains only one "a," then new words you come up with must contain no more than one "a." However, you may use the "a" in more than one word. You will have 5 minutes to come up with as many words as possible.*

Call time at the end of 5 minutes. Explain to the students that in the second round of the activity, they are to follow the same rules, however, this time they will be working together as a team. Assign each team a new word from the list. Again, allow 5 minutes for brainstorming and then call time.

Poll the teams to find out how many words they came up with while working alone and how many they came up with working as a team. (Chances are the team efforts produced more words.) Hold a culminating discussion. Encourage the students to hypothesize as to why they obtained the results they reported.

Discussion Questions:
1. How did you feel when you were working alone?
2. How did you feel when you were part of a team?
3. Under which circumstances — alone or with a team — did you produce more words? Under which circumstances did you enjoy yourself more?
4. Why do team efforts often produce better results than individual efforts?
5. If you prefer working with a team, what are some things you can do to make yourself more effective when you work

Interdependence Day!
Game Series and Discussion

Objectives:
The students will:
—play a series of cooperative games.
—demonstrate interdependence through play.

Materials:
for "Stack Up," as many chairs as players, except for the leader; none for the remainder of the games

Directions:
These games are useful in contrasting cooperative behaviors with competitive behaviors and for developing interdependence. Play them on a grassy outdoor area or indoors with plenty of tumbling mats — as a series or interspersed among other activities. If your group is large, go over the directions with everyone first, then break into smaller teams. After all of the games have been played, lead a follow-up discussion.

Game 1: "The Lap Game"

Players:
8 minimum, no maximum

Directions:
Players line up facing the same direction, hands on the waist of the person in front of them. The last player in line releases her hands from the person in front of her and lies down on her back with her feet on the ground and her knees bent. The next to the last person carefully backs up and sits on the last player's raised knees. The next person up the line then moves backwards and sits on the lap of the next to last person, and so on until everyone is sitting on the lap of the person behind. The larger the group, the more challenging it is to have everyone sitting at the same time. Players can also line up in a tight circle and all try to sit at the same time without anyone falling.

Game 2: "Stack Up"

Players:
6 or more

Directions:
One player is selected to be the "Caller." All remaining players sit in chairs in a circle. The Caller's job is to ask a series of questions of the group. If a player's answer is, "No," he remains in his chair. If a player's answer is, "Yes," she moves one seat to the right, regardless of whether or not someone is sitting in the chair. If someone is in the chair, she simply sits on that person's lap. The Caller asks questions such as, "Do you like broccoli?," "Were you born in this state?," "Do you have a dog?," "Are there younger brothers or sisters in your family?" The Caller tries to second guess the answers of the players so that they all end up in one chair on each other's lap. For example, the Caller might ask questions with obvious answers like, "Do you like free time?," "Would you rather have a new Ferrari than an old Plymouth?," "Do you like chocolate better than licorice?" When the Caller succeeds in manipulating the questions so that everyone is stacked up, a new game begins.

Game 3: "Caterpillar"

Players:
many, but a minimum of 10

Directions:
All players lie down side-by-side on their stomachs, as close together as possible, and with their arms outstretched over their heads. A player at one end of the row begins to roll over all the other players. He continues rolling until he reaches the end of the bodies, where he once again lies on his stomach, becoming the end person. Then the next person begins rolling across the bodies. When she is about halfway across the row of bodies, a third person may begin to roll. As the rolling proceeds, players initiate their rolls as soon as they are first in line, creating a caterpillar-like movement across the ground. When players run out of space, reverse the movement of the caterpillar.

Continued, next page

Game 4: "Lean-To"

Players:
8 or more

Directions:
All players join hands in a circle, the more the better. Players count off by two's ("one, two, one, two," etc.). An odd person may step inside the circle and become the "Caller." Otherwise, any player can become the Caller. When the Caller says, "Lean-to," the 1's slowly lean inward and the 2's lean outward. With hands held tightly, they should form an equally balanced "lean-to." This move may take a little practice to perfect. When it is accomplished to everyone's satisfaction, the Caller says, "Lean-to" again and the players switch leaning positions, the 2's leaning inward and the 1's leaning outward. When the players find switching back and forth easy, they can add the extra challenge of a "Left" or "Right" rotating movement.

Game 5: "Centipede"

Players:
4 or more

Directions:
Players sit down on the grass, one behind the other. Each player wraps her legs around the waist of the player in front of her to form the body of the centipede. Each player's arms become a set of legs for the centipede. When someone gives a signal, all players lift themselves off the ground with their hands and scoot along, like a giant centipede. Anyone who disconnects must shout, "Stop! Reconnect" and everyone waits for that person to reconnect. Large groups may divide into teams, making two or more centipedes, and race between a start and finish line. Centipedes may also decide on a "team noise" to make while scuttling across the field.

Discussion Questions:
1. Which game did you like best and why?
2. Which game would you like to change and how would you change it?
3. Who was the winner in these games? Explain.
4. When one or more players didn't cooperate or do their part, what effect did their behavior have on the game as a whole? ...on other players' enjoyment of the game?

Connect!
A Cooperative Team Experience

Objectives:
The students will:
—cooperate in solving a problem.
—identify specific cooperative and competitive behaviors and describe how they affect completion of a team task.

Materials:
construction paper or tag board (one color only) with which to make a set of puzzle pieces for each group of players (see "Preparation," below); table and chairs for each group of players

Preparation:
Start with <u>eight</u> 8-inch by 8-inch squares of construction paper or tag board *for each team*. Individually cut each square into three to five smaller pieces (see illustration). Place all of the pieces for one team in a single envelope.

Directions:
If the entire class is playing, ask the students to form teams of five to eight. Have each team sit around a table, and select one member to be its Observer. Announce that all other team members are players.

Take the Observers aside and say to them: *Your job is to stand beside the table while your team is playing the game and notice what happens. Be prepared to describe such things as how well the group works together, who shares puzzle parts and who does not; who makes an effort to include everyone and who does not; whether members concentrate only on the puzzle in front of them or watch the progress of all the puzzles; cooperative vs. competitive behaviors; any conflicts that occur and how they are resolved; who provides leadership.*

Read aloud the following rules of play:
- Your task is to assemble eight squares of EQUAL size.
- There will be NO talking, pointing, or other nonverbal communication.
- A player may pass puzzle parts to any other team member at any time.
- You may NOT take, ask for, or indicate in any way that you want another team member's puzzle pieces.
- There is no time limit. The game is over when you have finished the task.

Distribute the puzzle pieces randomly among the players. Give each player approximately the same number of pieces.

Give the signal to start play.

At the conclusion of play, have the Observers give feedback to their team. If several teams are playing, have the Observers do this simultaneously. Advise the teams to listen carefully, and not to interrupt, argue with, or put down the Observer.

Discussion Questions:
1. What did you learn from your Observer?
2. What was the object of the game?
3. Which kind of behavior was most effective in this game, cooperative or competitive? Why?
4. What are some of the effects of competitive behavior on a team? ...of cooperative behavior?
5. If anyone emerged as a leader in your group, how did that person demonstrate his or her leadership since there was no talking?
5. If you could play the game again, would you change your own behavior?
6. What did you learn from this experience?

Alphabet Names
Testing Team Synergy

Objectives:

The students will:

—compare the feelings, performance, and commitment levels experienced when performing a task alone and in small groups.

—describe how individual motivation affects individual performance.

—describe how individual and group motivation affects group synergy.

Materials:

individual writing materials, and one sheet of chart paper and magic marker for each small group

Directions:

Have each student take out a sheet of paper. Instruct the students to list the letters of the alphabet from "A" through "Z" in a vertical column down the left side of the sheet.

Randomly select a sentence from any document and read aloud the first twenty-six letters in that sentence. Tell the students to write these letters in a second vertical column to the right of the first. Every student should end up with the same twenty-six sets of letters.

Tell the students that they now have 10 minutes to individually record the names of famous people whose initials correspond with the twenty-six sets of letters. The people can be politicians, authors, inventors, film stars, musicians, etc. Only one name may be recorded for each set of initials. Announce that the maximum score is twenty-six points, one for each legitimate name.

At the end of 10 minutes, have the students exchange and "grade" each other's papers. Allow a few moments to verify any questionable names. Then have the students call out their scores while you jot them on the board. Circle the high score and ask the students to see who can be the first to compute and call out the average score. Write the average on the board, too.

Have the students form teams of five to eight. Give each team a sheet of chart paper and a magic marker. Have each team choose a recorder. Announce that, working together as a team, the students have 10 minutes to develop a second list of famous names. Have the recorder list the letters of the alphabet in a vertical column on the chart paper; then read the first 26 letters from a newly selected passage of text.

Call time after 10 minutes and check the lists. Record the team scores and average score on the board. Compare them with the individual scores. Then lead a discussion, focusing on the differences in motivation, frustration, enjoyment, and achievement experienced working individually and in teams.

Discussion Questions:
1. How did your individual score compare with your team score?
2. What feelings did you have working individually? ...working with a team?
3. How well did your team work together?
4. Which did you experience most when working individually, a sense of competition or collaboration? Why?
5. Which (competition or collaboration) did you experience most when working with a team? Why?
6. Were you more motivated to think of names when you were working alone or as part of a team? Why?
7. What did you learn from this activity?

Stepping Stones
Group Task and Discussion

Objectives:
The students will:
—work cooperatively in teams to solve a problem.
—identify effective and ineffective team behaviors.

Materials:
nine baseball bases (or any suitable substitute, such as cardboard squares or flattened paper bags) and an area (lawn, gym, or multipurpose room) at least 37 1/2 feet long.

Directions:
Measure off 37 1/2 feet and mark both ends of the space. Group the class into teams of no more than ten and no fewer than seven each. (For example, 31 students could be divided into three groups of eight and one group of seven.) Allow *one less* stepping stone than there are team members. Subtract 2 1/2 feet from the length of the space for every team member *less than ten*, as follows:

> 9 team members = 35 feet
> 8 team members = 32 1/2 feet
> 7 team members = 30 feet

Explain to the students that you would like them to imagine that between the two markers there is a raging river. Their task is to get each team member across the river, using the bases as stepping stones.

As each team attempts to cross the river, members must decide how to use their stepping stones to best advantage. This task involves trial, error, and team cooperation. Team members will need to experiment and help one another.

While the first team attempts to cross the river, the other teams should go to another room so that they cannot watch. This will allow each team to approach the problem without having seen another team work on it. On the other hand, do allow teams that have completed the task to watch the next teams attempt it. Laughter and encouragement on the part of observers will make the activity fun and interesting, but do not allow students to make derogatory statements or sounds.

Discussion Questions:

1. What was the toughest part of this exercise for you?
2. What part did you enjoy most?
3. How did your team work together? Did a leader emerge? How were problems resolved?
4. What did your team do that proved particularly effective? ...ineffective?
5. What did you see another team do that seemed particularly effective? ...ineffective?
6. What did you learn about teamwork from this activity?

Protect Your Rights!
Developing a Classroom Bill of Rights

Objectives:
The students will:
—explain how knowing one another's rights prevents conflict.
—develop and vote on a *Classroom Bill of Rights*.

Materials:
a display copy of the *U.S. Bill of Rights*; writing materials for the students

Directions:
Begin with a class discussion on the U.S. Constitution's *Bill of Rights*. Display a list of the rights, and talk about each one. Point out that the primary reason our country has a *Bill of Rights* is to help preserve and protect the individual rights of its citizens.

Announce that the students are going to draw up a Classroom Bill of Rights to help protect the individual rights of themselves and you, and to help prevent conflicts resulting from violations of those rights.

Brainstorm a list of areas in which written rights might be appropriate and helpful. Record suggested items on the chalkboard. For example, the students might want to develop written rights in the following areas:
- expression of feelings
- expression of beliefs and opinions
- giving and receiving respect
- respect of property (e.g., desk and contents)
- work and study
- quiet and privacy
- help and assistance
- violence and peer pressure
- fair hearing in conflict situations

Have the students form committees of four to six. Divide the categories among the committees, and ask the committees to develop written rights for each of their areas. Suggest that they start by selecting a chairperson and recorder.

Have the chairpersons form a special delegation whose job it is to combine the lists, eliminate duplications, make necessary changes, and then submit a final draft to the class for approval. Examine and discuss each proposed right with the students and vote to approve, disapprove, or recommend that it receive further study and work. Return items requiring further work to their original committees. If a suggested right is at odds with school policy, explain the problem and return it to committee.

Have volunteers record the final *Classroom Bill of Rights* on chart paper for display in the classroom.

Discussion Questions:
1. What are "rights" and how do we get them?
2. Which of the rights we've developed are most important to you and why?
3. How will having a *Classroom Bill of Rights* help prevent conflict? How will it help resolve conflict?
4. If someone in the class violates one of your rights, what can you do about it?

Extension:
Involve the entire school in the project. Have classes appoint a representative to each of the established committees. Hold a constitutional convention to finalize and ratify the *School Bill of Rights*.

A Time I Worked in a Successful Group
A Circle Session

Objectives:
The students will:
—describe characteristics of a successful group.
—describe their contributions to the success of a group.
—state that a successful group needs the diverse abilities of all its members.

Introduce the Topic:
All of us have belonged to a group that has had some form of success. Successful groups have certain characteristics in common. One of these characteristics is interdependence. Interdependence exists when the strength of the group is built on the contributions of its members and the members derive benefits from being part of the group. Today, we are going to look at an experience of our own to explore the characteristic of interdependence. In the process, we're going to discover some other characteristics of successful groups. Our topic is, "A Time I Worked in a Successful Group."

Think of one time when you were a part of a group that achieved something significant. The group might have been a team, or a work group with a particular task to complete. Maybe it was a family group, or a social or religious group. It might even have been a bunch of friends working together. Whatever the group, focus on its achievements. What made the group successful? What were some of the characteristics of the group that caused it to function so well? How did you feel when you were part of this group. Take a moment to think about all of these things. The topic is, "A Time I Worked in a Successful Group."

Discussion Questions:

1. How did members of the group feel toward one another?
2. What were some of the contributions that different people made to the success of the groups we discussed?
3. In what ways can groups outperform individuals?
4. Under what circumstances can individuals accomplish more alone?
5. What are some characteristics besides interdependence that make groups successful?

We Used Teamwork to Get It Done
A Circle Session

Objectives:
The students will:
—describe a real situation in which a goal was attained through teamwork.
—identify characteristics of a functioning team.
—describe the effects of teamwork on individual commitment and motivation.

Introduce the Topic:

Today, we're going to talk about teamwork and what it can accomplish. Our topic is, "We Used Teamwork to Get It Done."

Think of a situation in which you worked with a team of people to accomplish a goal. You can share something about a team activity in which you've participated here in class, or some other team experience you've had recently. Perhaps you belong to an athletic or debate team that won a competition. Maybe your family worked as a team to clean up the house or hold a yard sale. Or you and some friends may have done something together, like cook a meal, plan a party, or hold a car wash. Tell us what the team was trying to accomplish and how you felt being part of it. Take a few moments to think about it. The topic is, "We Used Teamwork to Get It Done."

Discussion Questions:
1. How did most of us feel about being part of a team?
2. What makes a team work well together?
3. How does the saying, "The whole is more than the sum of its parts," apply to teams?
4. How does working with a team on a school assignment affect the quality of your work?
5. How does it affect your motivation?
6. How would you characterize the differences between a group and a team?

More Products from Innerchoice Publishing

TEACHING THE SKILLS OF CONFLICT RESOLUTION
Activities and Strategies for Counselors and Teachers

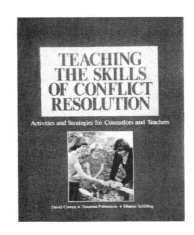

Conflict is an inevitable element in every school day, and as a counselor or teacher you are frequently its mediator. This thoroughly useful activity book will help you reduce conflict through the creation of a more peaceful, cooperative learning environment, and resolve and learn from conflict when it occurs. Activities help students deal with their **feelings**; appreciate and include others; practice effective **communication**, **problem-solving** and **decision-making**; reduce **stress**, and learn **peer mediation skills**. Conflict resolution strategies incorporate *negotiation, compromise, active listening, apologizing, soliciting intervention, postponing, distracting, abandoning, exaggerating, humor, chance, sharing,* and many more. Students examine personal and interpersonal conflicts and proceed to school, local, and global problems.

IMPACT!
A Self-Esteem Based Skill Development Program for Secondary Students

This exceptional program-in-a-kit facilitates the growth of secondary students in the social and emotional domains by teaching skills that are essential to self-esteem. *IMPACT!* is an ideal tool for counselors, and may be integrated by teachers into virtually any subject area, infusing the regular curriculum with life skills and personal relevancy. *IMPACT!* increases the ability of students to function effectively in a multicultural environment, and encourages them to recognize their broader role as members of society. The curriculum guide includes units on *communicating effectively, self-awareness, making decisions, resolving conflicts, taking responsibility, managing stress, setting and attaining goals, solving problems, relating to peers, team building,* and *careers*. Features the circle session discussion process and many experiential activities, along with theory information, and individualized worksheets (available separately in Spanish). Kit includes a second book containing additional circle session topics, and the Circle Session Rules Poster.